The Myth of Nations

The Myth of Nations

The Medieval Origins
of Europe

Patrick J. Geary

PRINCETON UNIVERSITY PRESS   PRINCETON AND OXFORD

Copyright © 2002 by Princeton University Press
Published by Princeton University Press, 41 William Street,
Princeton, New Jersey 08540
In the United Kingdom: Princeton University Press,
3 Market Place, Woodstock, Oxfordshire OX20 1SY

All Rights Reserved

Library of Congress Cataloging-in-Publication Data

Geary, Patrick J., 1948–
  The myth of nations : the medieval origins of Europe / Patrick J. Geary.
    p.   cm.
  Includes bibliographical references and index.
  ISBN 0-691-09054-8
  1. Europe—Ethnic relations—History. 2. Rome—Boundaries—History.
3. Nationalism—Europe—History—19th century. 4. Immigrants—Europe.
5. Rome—History—Germanic Invasions, 3rd–6th centuries. 6. Xenopho-
bia—Europe. 7. Europe—Race relations. I. Title.
D135 .G43   2001
305.8′0094—dc21

                                                          2001036336

This book has been composed in Baskerville with Stone Sans display

Printed on acid-free paper. ∞

www.pup.princeton.edu

Printed in the United States of America

10 9 8 7 6 5 4 3 2 1

For Jean Airiau and Jim Usdan

DEDICATED FRIENDS AND DEDICATED READERS WHO UNDERSTAND THE
IMPORTANCE OF THE PAST FOR THE PRESENT AND THE DIFFERENCE
BETWEEN THE TWO

Contents

CONTENTS

Acknowledgments

My reflections on the relationship between the myths of European peoples and the realities of contemporary nationalism have developed in dialogue with many people, especially my students and colleagues at the University of Florida, UCLA, the University of Notre Dame, and the Central European University in Budapest. During the academic years 1994–1996, the UCLA Center for Medieval and Renaissance Studies conducted a series of conversations on the topic "Creating Ethnicity: The Abuse of History," sponsored by the National Endowment for the Humanities. In the course of these conferences, I was able to refine my understanding of the relationship between the distant past and the present. As a guest participant in meetings of the European Science Foundation's project, "The Transformation of the Roman World," I was privileged to interact with a wide spectrum of European scholars who are at the forefront of understanding the transformations of ethnic groups in Late Antiquity.

ACKNOWLEDGMENTS

After deciding to try to share what I had learned about past ethnicities with a general audience, I turned to many colleagues and friends for their assistance. Through the years, Otto Johnston, James Turner, and Robert Sullivan were especially helpful in clarifying the background of nineteenth-century Europe. Stephen Fireman introduced me to the complexities of African ethnogenesis and János Bak taught me much about the realities of life in Central Europe in the twentieth century. I am particularly grateful to Herwig Wolfram, Walter Pohl, Hans Hummer, and James Usdan, each of whom read early drafts of this manuscript and offered their insights and suggestions. Brigitta Van Rheinberg worked mightly to help make this book accessible to the audience for which it is intended—nonacademics who wonder about the relationship between past and present. Holly J. Grieco assisted me in preparing the manuscript. What may be of value in this book largely comes from these generous scholars and friends. The errors that remain are mine.

Patrick J. Geary
Los Angeles

The Myth of Nations

The Crisis of European Identity

Just a few short years ago, when Western Europeans looked to the future, their thoughts were almost entirely on the full implementation of the European Community's economic and financial reforms of 1992. Some awaited with relish the prospect of currency unification, the elimination of internal tariffs, and the free circulation of citizens. Others did so with hesitation or even fear. Still, by and large, the nations of the Community saw the problems facing Europe in a particularly narrow perspective. First, they took a remarkably parochial view of what constituted Europe. Second, they saw their challenges relating more to the economic problems of the future than to the emotionally explosive problems of the past. The very name of their organization betrayed the comfortable myopia that the postwar political configuration had made possible. The "European Community" was no such thing. It was actually the Western European Community, to which the addition of Greece had already created considerable problems. For these nations, "Europe" stopped at the so-called Iron Curtain: Beyond that lay the Warsaw Pact nations, poor but blessedly distant cousins,

1

largely irrelevant to the economic and, increasingly, even to the military concerns of the Community.

Within this "little Europe," the old problems of nationalism, economic competition, and social tensions seemed, if not entirely solved, then at least manageable. Separatist movements in Northern Ireland, Corsica, and northern Spain continued to shed blood, but these were limited in scope and geographically isolated. Elsewhere, as in the South Tyrol, Brittany, and Catalonia, the micronationalist movements of the 1970s had largely devolved into folkloric tourist attractions. Even the antagonisms between Walloons and Flemings in Belgium had subsided, as Brussels moved forward as the capital of the Community. National boundaries, for centuries *causae belli,* had not only been fixed by treaties and guaranteed by the Helsinki Accords, but, with implementation of the 1992 program, they seemed destined to become irrelevant. England continued to be uncertain about whether it wanted to be part of Europe, but the rest of the United Kingdom had no such hesitation, and the "Chunnel" promised to unite France and England in a manner that would permanently end the island's geographical and psychological isolation. After four decades of irritating military and economic dependence on the United States, the European Community was about to emerge as an equal partner in world affairs, challenging not only a faltering United States but a mighty Japan as the dominant economic power. In the Brave New World that was to be the Europe of 1992, the old problems of nationalism simply had no place.

How incredibly naive such a view now seems. In a few tumultuous months, that Iron Curtain, which had not only isolated the East but sheltered the West, rose to reveal a vast and profoundly dangerous Europe that stretched east to the Urals. The initial wildly enthusiastic reaction on the part of Western democracies soon turned to dismay and fear as wave after wave of seismic shocks rolling out of Moscow irrevocably altered the political landscape

2

of Europe, in place since the end of the Second World War. At the same time, the effects of forty years of government policies to provide cheap labor in France and Germany and to settle the obligations of Empire in Great Britain touched off a crisis of identity and a xenophobic reaction in these Western democracies.

Nationalism, ethnocentricism, racism—specters long thought exorcised from the European soul—have returned with their powers enhanced by a half-century of dormancy. The last great European Empire, that of the Soviet Union, has crumbled into autonomy-minded republics, many of which are no more stable than the Union they sought to throw off. The once-formidable Warsaw Pact no longer exists, replaced by a series of struggling, debt-ridden polities, themselves torn by ethnic tensions and seeking a place in the New World Order. A united Germany is searching for a new identity, and shouts of "Germany for Germans" are heard in the streets. The Balkans, the powder keg of the last century, once more erupted into civil war. These extraordinary and continuing events have shaken the West no less profoundly than the East. The result is a deep crisis of identity, which raises the question of how Europeans see themselves, their societies, and their neighbors.

"How ironic, that at the end of the twentieth century, Central Europe appears just as it did at the end of the nineteenth." The truth of this remark, made by an Austrian historian in 1991, is even more evident today. In the Balkans and the Baltics, in Ukraine, in the Russias, in the Crimea, the ancient claims to national sovereignty are heard once more. Ethnic communities forced to live under the internationalist banner of socialism now find the freedom to renew ancient blood feuds. The intractable problems of minority rights, and religious and linguistic differences, which precipitated two world wars are once more at the forefront of European attention. Not only is communism discredited, but everything socialism opposed is now again in vogue. Not only does this mean that capitalism and individualism have become popular, but anti-Semitism, re-

3

ligious chauvinism, and atavistic racism as well. Polish politicians compete to see who is the most Polish; Hungarians renew their disputes with Romanians to the east and Slovaks to the north. Serbs and Croats kill each other and both kill Bosnians in the name of national rights. Serbs launched a massive attempt to eliminate Albanians from their sacred Kosovo, and, after the terrors of a NATO aerial war, Kosovars retaliated against the Serbian minority with the same brutality they had been shown by their former oppressors. Ethnic groups scattered across the corpse of the Soviet Union demanded the right of political self-determination. No one can yet say whether the horrors of Chechnya are precursors of future violence.

All these peoples inhabit areas that contain other ethnic minorities, and most also have members living as minorities within areas dominated by other peoples. As a result, demands for political autonomy based on ethnic identity will inevitably lead to border conflicts, suppression of minority rights, and civil strife, as each group goes about the grisly task of "ethnic cleansing" to ensure themselves of an ethnically homogeneous territorial state.

Even more troubling to political stability in the West than the potential for the rebirth of traditional regional separatist movements are the new ethnic minorities, particularly in Germany and France.

"The *Bundesrepublik* was a good fatherland," a German colleague told me with nostalgia and concern in 1990. Whether the new Germany will be as good to its children is unclear. The unification, combined with the presence in the united Germany of thousands of refugees from the East, has precipitated a crisis of proportions unprecedented in the last half-century, deeply affecting how majorities see themselves and others. The generation that created the German economic miracle is now entering retirement, and their children and grandchildren, raised in the comfort of the Bonn regime, do not seem eager to surrender a portion of the good life to their poor cousins in the East. What the Eastern Germans are receiving is the share of the Western economy previously granted to Germany's silent partners in the *Wirtschaftswunder:* the Turkish and Balkan "guestworkers" who are being pushed out of Germany and into France and Belgium by the crowds of eager German laborers from the former DDR. These latter, facing unemployment at home and largely low-level jobs in the western *Länder,* look with suspicion on the Turks and Slavs already established in Germany and with undisguised loathing on the Poles, Romanians, and others seeking a better life for themselves in the new Germany. In the meantime, the diversion of federal funds into the old East Germany away from the old Federal Republic creates antagonism and tensions on the part of those accustomed to a generous and supportive state system.

The extreme reaction is the rebirth of racist violence in the cities in the East. A less extreme but perhaps even more dangerous reaction is the renewed debate about who has the right to share in the German prosperity. Already, the German constitution allows for a "right of return," privileging descendants of German-speaking inhabitants of Eastern Europe, who have never seen Germany and may not speak any German, over Turks born and raised in Germany. Who is a German? Can an immigrant become German, or is German identity a matter of blood, of race? These questions have been asked before, with terrible consequences.

Germany is the most intimately involved in the transformation of Europe, but the German dilemma, while the most obvious, is by no means unique. In France, the presence of millions of Muslims—both descendants of North Africans and recently arrived immigrants, legal as well as clandestine—are leading to a reexamination of French national identity, with troubling results. Fear of the Islamization of France has led to a resurgence of the French xenophobic right, which now claims as supporters upwards of one-third of the popular electorate and for whom "French" is more a racial and cultural than a political category. In September 1991,

5

for example, former French president Valéry Giscard d'Estaing termed immigration into France an invasion and called for the substitution of the *droit du sang* (right of blood) in place of the *droit du sol* (right of soil) as the criterion for acquiring French citizenship.[1] At the same time, France and Belgium are attempting to cope with secondary refugees, pushed out of Germany, who must now compete with the millions of unemployed or underemployed North Africans. Italy and Greece have faced a flood of Albanian refugees, fleeing a destitute economy and a bankrupt political system. Austria, initially fearful of being drawn into the civil war on its border, is now attempting to cope with thousands of refugees and migrants from Romania, Bulgaria, and the former Yugoslavia. This country, which had long basked in the myth of "the first victim of Nazi aggression" while enjoying the status of neutral ground for the conduct of cold war interaction, has seen a party with strong chauvinistic and xenophobic elements emerge as the third largest political movement. Are the nations of the European Community "lands of immigration" or are the benefits of citizenship to be reserved for "real" French, Italians, Danes, and British? The very fact that such questions are being posed indicates how very much alive the discredited agenda of nationalism and racism remains.

If the current events in Europe draw the most attention, one must not forget that the rest of the world, and particularly the United States, are not immune to these ideological tendencies. While today many see the United States as a nation of polyethnic immigration, this has not always been the case, and significant portions of the political leadership continue to draw support by encouraging fears about the loss of a national identity closely tied to the English language and national tradition.[2] This is hardly surprising: Our third president, Thomas Jefferson, had originally wanted to place on the great seal of the United States replicas of Hengist and Horsa, the first Saxon chiefs to arrive in (and begin to conquer) Britain. Jefferson argued that it was Hengist and Horsa "from whom we claim the honor of being descended, and whose political principles and form of government we have assumed."[3] Through the late nineteenth century and the early twentieth century, racial Anglo-Saxonism as an ideology excluded Irish, southern Europeans, and Asians from America. Today, politicians of hate can ignite enthusiasm by raising the specter of an America where English is not the only official language.

A historian of the early Middle Ages, who observes this problem firsthand, who listens to the rhetoric of nationalist leaders, and who reads the scholarship produced by official or quasi-official historians, is immediately struck by how central the interpretation of the period from circa 400–1000 is to this debate. Suddenly, the history of Europe over a millennium ago is anything but academic: The interpretation of the period of the dissolution of the Roman Empire and the barbarian migration has become the fulcrum of political discourse across much of Europe.

In France, National Front leader Jean Marie Le Pen declares himself the champion of "the French people born with the baptism of Clovis in 496, who have carried this inextinguishable flame, which is the soul of a people, for almost one thousand five hundred years."[4] On June 28, 1989, the Serbian strongman Slobodan Milosevic organized an assembly, reportedly numbering more than a million people, on the "Kosovo polje," the "Blackbird Field," where on that same date in 1389 the Serbian army was defeated by the Ottoman Turks. His stated purpose: to reaffirm Serbian determination never to part with this disputed territory.[5] But the Albanian majority's claim could take precedence over that of the Serbs: The latter, after all, had only controlled Kosovo for less than three hundred years, that is, since conquering it from the Byzantines in the eleventh century. The former, by contrast, claim descent from the ancient Illyrians, the indigenous inhabitants of the region, and, thus, according to the same deadly logic, the people with "the best right" to Kosovo. Such claims and counterclaims led directly to the horrors of the Kosovar war, horrors by no means at an end as this book goes to press.

It is not only nationalist political leaders who play history for politics. Reputable scholars are drawn into the polemical uses of the past as well. In Transylvania—a region fortified by Hungarians in the eleventh century, settled by Saxons in the twelfth, ruled by the Turks, the Habsburgs, and the Hungarians, and, since 1920, a part of Romania—the debate about political legitimacy is couched in terms of ninth-century history and carried on in part by professional historians and archaeologists. Did the nomadic Magyar horsemen arrive in a region inhabited by a thriving "indigenous Roman" population or in one already laid waste by Slavic invaders? Romanians interpret the scant archaeological evidence to answer *yes,* claiming that their ancestors, the Vlachs, had inhabited this region since Roman times and, thus, in spite of a thousand years of interrupted rule, have a legitimate right to the region. Leading Hungarian archaeologists and historians, on the other hand, argue that the evidence suggests that, by the time that the Magyars arrived in the area, the remains of Roman society had long since disappeared and that, therefore, Transylvania should by rights belong to Hungary. Another example of how easily medieval scholarship is drawn into contemporary politics comes from the Austrian province of Carinthia, home of Austria's right-wing politician Jorg Heider. Are hill forts recently excavated in southeastern Carinthia evidence of sixth-century Slavic settlement or the remains of indigenous "Roman" defense works? When an Austrian archaeologist publicly supported the former hypothesis, he was cautioned against that view by rightist Carinthian political leaders who considered that such hypotheses lent political support to the notion that Slavs might have rights in Carinthia.

Such examples could be multiplied across Europe. Early medieval historians, not accustomed to being at the center of political debate, find their period of history suddenly pivotal in a contest for the past and their rhetoric being used to lay claims to the present and the future.

Unfortunately, policy makers and even most scholars of both East and West generally know very little about this period and even less about the actual process of ethnogenesis that brought European societies into existence. Probably no other period of history is as obscure and obscured by nationalist and chauvinist scholarship. This very obscurity makes it easy prey for ethnic nationalist propaganda: Claims can be based on the appropriation of the migration period with impunity, since few people know any better. Once the premises projected onto this period have been accepted, political leaders can draw out policy implications to suit their political agenda.

These demands, justified by reference to ethnic migrations of Late Antiquity and long-vanished medieval kingdoms, threaten not only the political entities of the East but those of the West as well. Can the European Community recognize the "rights" of the Lithuanians but not those of the Corsicans? Can it condemn the aggression of the Serbs against the Bosnians but not that of the English against the Irish or the Spanish against the Basques? If the Moldavians and Slovenes have the right to their own sovereign state, why not the Flemings, the Catalans, and the Sorbs? If long-integrated regions of the Soviet Union, such as Belorussia, can suddenly find a national consciousness, is this not also possible for Bavaria, Brittany, Friesland, Sardinia, and Scotland?

Many fear that the scenes broadcast from Brindisi of thousands of rioting Albanian refugees and the images from Berlin of Romanian Gypsies begging in the streets are but an avatar of Giscard d'Estaing's invasion of desperate peoples from the East, driven by hunger, civil war, and anarchy toward the West, a vast migration or *Völkerwanderung* of the sort Western Europe has not known for a thousand years. For the present, at least, the Kosovars have been able to return from their refugee camps in Albania and Macedonia to Kosovo. Will the next "people" driven from their ancestral homes by ethnic hatred and modern weaponry be as fortunate, or will their hosts find them permanent and increasingly unwelcome guests?

And yet, in the history of Europe, such mass movements have been the rule rather than the exception. The present populations of Europe, with their many languages, traditions, and cultural and political identities, are the result of these waves of migrations. First came bands of peoples, probably speaking what are known as Indo-European languages, who replaced or absorbed the indigenous populations of Greece, the Balkans, and Italy. The Celts, another Indo-European people came next, spreading from what is today Czechoslovakia, Austria, and southern Germany and Switzerland to Ireland in the sixth century B.C.E., pushing back, absorbing, or eradicating the indigenous European population until the only survivors were the Basques of southern France and northern Spain. From the first century B.C.E., Germanic peoples began pushing the Celts from the east to the Rhine, but they and the Celts confronted a different invader: the expanding Roman Empire, which conquered and Romanized much of Europe as it did Asia Minor and North Africa. New migrations of Germanic and Central Asian peoples began in the third century, eventually replacing the Roman imperial system with a mosaic of separate kingdoms. In the East, bands of Slavs filtered into the Alps, the Carpathian Basin, the Balkans, and Greece. The last major population influxes of the first millennium were the arrival of the Magyars in the Danubian plain and the Scandinavians in Normandy and northern England. Although many scholars pretend that the "Migration Period" ended with the end of the first millennium, its final phase actually came with the arrival of Turkic peoples in Greece and the Balkans in the thirteenth through the sixteenth centuries. Now, at the dawn of the third millennium, Europe still lives with the consequences of this migration period, while fearing yet another. The parallels are being explicitly drawn. In an article appearing in *Le Monde,* the French journalist and commentator Claude Allègre suggested that one need only read my own *Before France and Germany,* perversely subtitled by the marketing department of the French publisher *The Birth of France (Naissance de la France),* to see "how presumably controlled immigration . . . caused a world which seemed indestructible to explode violently from within."[6] Presumably, some want to see contemporary history as a re-enactment of the fall of the Roman Empire and hope to find in the lessons of the past a means of preventing contemporary European civilization from being destroyed by new barbarian hordes.

Any historian who has spent much of his career studying this earlier period of ethnic formation and migration can only look upon the development of politically conscious nationalism and racism with apprehension and disdain, particularly when these ideologies appropriate and pervert history as their justification. This pseudo-history assumes, first, that the peoples of Europe are distinct, stable and objectively identifiable social and cultural units, and that they are distinguished by language, religion, custom, and national character, which are unambiguous and immutable. These peoples were supposedly formed either in some impossibly remote moment of prehistory, or else the process of ethnogenesis took place at some moment during the Middle Ages, but then ended for all time.

Second, ethnic claims demand the political autonomy of all persons belonging to a particular ethnic group and at the same time the right of that people to govern its historic territory, usually defined in terms of early medieval settlements or kingdoms, regardless of who may now live in it. This double standard allows Lithuanians to repress Poles and Russians, even as they demand their own autonomy, and Serbs to claim both historically "Serbian" areas of Bosnia inhabited by Muslims and areas of Croatia inhabited by Serbs. It also allows the Irish Republican Army to demand major-

11

ity rule in southern Ireland and minority rule in the North. Implicit in these claims is that there was a moment of "primary acquisition," the first century for the Germans, the fifth for the Franks, the sixth and seventh centuries for the Croats, the ninth and tenth for the Hungarians, and so on, which established once and for all the geographical limits of legitimate ownership of land. After these moments of primary acquisition, according to this circular reasoning, similar subsequent migrations, invasions, or political absorptions have all been illegitimate. In many cases, this has meant that fifteen hundred years of history is to be obliterated.

Equally disturbing is the very great extent to which the international community, including even pluralistic societies such as the United States, accepts the basic premises that peoples exist as objective phenomena and that the very existence of a people gives it the right to self-government. In other words, we assume that, somehow, political and cultural identity are and have a right to be, united. Surely, if Lithuanians or Croats have their own language, their own music, and their own dress, then they have a right to their own parliament and their own army. True, the international community must attempt to limit the inevitable consequences of ancient ethnic antagonisms, such as inter-ethnic warfare, but the principle of the ancient right of ethnic self-government is hardly questioned. Indeed, one can go still further: The claims to ancient ethnic rights and inherited blood feuds are useful to isolationists both in America and Western Europe. If these people have "always" hated each other, if their identities and their antagonisms are fixed and immutable, then intervention in the hope of settling these wars is futile. By embracing the rhetoric of ethnic nationalism, even while confessing to abhor it, the rest of the world can justify the creation of ethnically "pure" nations as the only alternative to genocide.

Actually, there is nothing particularly ancient about either the peoples of Europe or their supposed right to political autonomy.

The claims to sovereignty that Europe is seeing in Eastern and Central Europe today are a creation of the nineteenth century, an age that combined the romantic political philosophies of Rousseau and Hegel with "scientific" history and Indo-European philology to produce ethnic nationalism. This pseudoscience has destroyed Europe twice and may do so yet again. Europe's peoples have always been far more fluid, complex, and dynamic than the imaginings of modern nationalists. Names of peoples may seem familiar after a thousand years, but the social, cultural, and political realities covered by these names were radically different from what they are today. For this reason we need a new understanding of the peoples of Europe, especially in that formative period of European identity that was the first millennium. We also need to understand how the received tradition, which has summoned millions of people into the streets and sent millions more to their graves in the twentieth century, took form a little more than a century ago.

The following chapters attempt to present an overview of this new understanding. We shall start with a brief examination of the origins of modern ethnic nationalism and modern historical studies in the eighteenth and nineteenth centuries. Then we shall examine briefly the development of intellectual and cultural categories by which Europeans have distinguished and categorized themselves from the fifth century B.C.E. until Late Antiquity. Only then will we be ready to examine the historical circumstances within which the "peoples of Europe" developed in that crucial period that was Late Antiquity and the early Middle Ages, that pseudo "moment of primary acquisition," which once more looms large in European mythology and which has come to be one of the guiding principles when dealing with "ethnic" issues worldwide. No one should be so naive as to expect that a clearer understanding of the formation of Europe's peoples will ease nationalist tensions or limit the hatred and bloodshed that they continue to cause. At best, one hopes that those who are being called upon to assist in the actualization of demands based on these appropriations of history, whether in Europe, the Middle East, or elsewhere, will be more skeptical of them. Failing even this, historians have a duty to speak out, even if they are certain to be ignored.

A Poisoned Landscape: Ethnicity and Nationalism in the Nineteenth Century

Modern history was born in the nineteenth century, conceived and developed as an instrument of European nationalism. As a tool of nationalist ideology, the history of Europe's nations was a great success, but it has turned our understanding of the past into a toxic waste dump, filled with the poison of ethnic nationalism, and the poison has seeped deep into popular consciousness. Cleaning up this waste is the most daunting challenge facing historians today.

The real history of the nations that populated Europe in the early Middle Ages begins not in the sixth century but in the eighteenth. This is not to deny that people living in the distant past had a sense of nation or collective identity. But the past two centuries of intellectual activity and political confrontation have so utterly changed the ways we think about social and political groups that we cannot pretend to provide an "objective" view of early medieval social categories, unencumbered by this recent past. Not only is ethnic nationalism, as we currently understand it, in a certain sense an invention of this recent period, but, as we shall see, the very tools of analysis by which we pretend to practice scientific history were invented and perfected within a wider climate of nationalism and nationalist preoccupations. Rather than neutral instruments of scholarship, the modern methods of researching and writing history were developed specifically to further nationalist aims. Since both the object and method of investigation are suspect, it is only fair to recognize the subjective nature of our investigation at the outset by briefly reviewing the process that led to their invention.

Ethnic Nationalism and the Age of Revolution

The story of the emergence of nationalism in the eighteenth century and the early nineteenth century has been told many times. The ethnically based nation-states of today have been described as "imagined communities," called into being by the creative efforts of nineteenth-century intellectuals and politicians, who transformed earlier, romantic, nationalist traditions into political programs.[1] Indeed, a rash of books and articles—some scholarly, others aimed at a general public—argue that many "age-old traditions," from national identities to Scottish plaids, are the recent and cynical invention of politicians or entrepreneurs. There is much truth to this characterization, especially since it draws attention to the formative role played in the recent past by individuals and groups in the elaboration of supposedly ancient ideologies. At the same time, however, it would be absurd to suggest that, because these communities are in some sense "imagined," they should be dismissed or trivialized, or to imply that "somehow imagined" is synonymous either with "imaginary" or "insignificant." First, while the specific forms of ethnically based nation-states of today may indeed have been called into being by the efforts of

16

nineteenth-century romantics and nationalists, this does not mean that other forms of imagining nations did not exist in the past—forms equally powerful as, even if very different from, those of the modern world. Nineteenth-century scholars, politicians, and poets did not simply make up the past; they drew on pre-existing traditions, written sources, legends, and beliefs, even if they used them in new ways to forge political unity or autonomy. Second, even if these communities are in a sense imagined, they are very real and very powerful: All important historical phenomena are in some sense psychological, and mental phenomena—from religious extremism to political ideology—have probably killed more people than anything but the Black Death.

The specific process through which nationalism emerged as a potent political ideology has varied by region across Europe and well beyond. In regions lacking political organization, such as Germany, nationalism provided an ideology to create and augment state power. In large states, such as France and Great Britain, governments and ideologues ruthlessly suppressed minority languages, cultural traditions, and variant memories of the past, in favor of a unified national history and homogeneous language and culture that could claim to extend far into the past. In polyethnic empires, such as those of the Ottomans or Habsburgs, individuals identifying themselves as members of oppressed minorities used nationalism to claim the right not only to a separate cultural existence but also, as a consequence, to political autonomy.

A fairly typical version of how the ideology of nationalism gives rise to independence movements, particularly in Eastern and Central Europe, posits three stages in the process of creating these imagined communities.[2] They include, first, the study of the language, culture, and history of a subject people by a small group of "awakened" intellectuals; second, the transmission of the scholars' ideas by a group of "patriots" who disseminate them throughout society; and finally, the stage at which the national movement

17

reaches its mass apogee.[3] With minor variations, this process can be traced from Germany in the eighteenth century across much of the Ottoman, Habsburg, and Russian empires in the nineteenth century, and, ultimately, to colonial and postcolonial Asia, Africa, and the Americas in the twentieth century.

Most students of nationalism would not dispute this general description of the process of national awakening and politicization. Hotly disputed, however, is whether the original reflection by "awakened" intellectuals merely acknowledges a pre-existing and repressed people or if these intellectuals invent the very people that they study. The historian of Croatia, Ivo Banac, for example, differs from many when he argues that "In order to be accepted, an ideology must proceed from reality. Nationalism can attempt to deal with the conditions of its group's subjugation, but it cannot manufacture the conditions."[4] At one level he is certainly correct: If individuals do not experience subjugation and discrimination, promises of remedies are unlikely to be effective. However, understood in a different sense, such a formulation is potentially dangerous: It implies that the groups—potential nations, as it were—exist even before intellectuals recognize them; that the conditions of subjugation are peculiar to a given group; and that nationalism is the appropriate cure for these ills. In other words, while nationalism may not create the conditions, it can certainly manufacture the nation itself. In the nineteenth century, under the influence of revolution and romanticism, and with the apparent failure of the old aristocratic order in the political arena, intellectuals and politicians created new nations, nations that they then projected into the distant past of the early Middle Ages.

The intellectual context in which modern nationalism was born was initially the fascination with the ancient world on the part of European scholarly elites, particularly in France and Germany. Fascination with classical culture and civilization—cultivated especially in the Netherlands and then in France and in German universities such as Göttingen—set the stage for a radical reversal of self-perceptions and identity, sweeping away centuries of very different social identities.

Group Identity Before Nationalism

During the high Middle Ages and the early Renaissance, "nation"—along with religion, kindred, lordship, and social stratum—provided one of the overlapping ways by which politically active elites identified themselves and organized collaborative action. However, a sense of belonging to a nation did not constitute the most important of these bonds. Nor did a common national identity unite the high and low, lord and peasant, into a deeply felt community of interest. Even less did intellectuals and social elites find their primary self-identification by projecting their national identities into a distant past of the migration period. Rather, to the extent that they looked to the ancient past for solidarity, they identified self-consciously with Roman society and culture.

Progressively, however, from the Renaissance on, European intellectuals in France, Germany, and Eastern Europe began to identify with the victims of Roman imperialist expansion, the Gauls, the Germans, or the Slavs. This transformation of identity took place within political contexts that determined their directions. In Renaissance France, which experienced tremendous continuity in its monarchy, the reality of the state was never in doubt but the existence of a single French people was. In Germany, ever since the ninth century, authors occasionally spoke of a German people, but, in the absence of a unified German state, the identification of a German cultural tradition did not necessarily demand a corresponding political tradition. In other areas, such as Poland, a "national" sense was claimed as the exclusive domain of the aristocracy, who felt little, if any, solidarity with the peasants who worked their lands.

19

French theses concerning the identity of the French developed within the context of royal absolutism and aristocratic or popular opposition. The right to rule was disputed between the king and the nobility, or first estate. Both king and nobility based their claims on the assertion that, since the time of Julius Caesar, the commoners, or third estate, constituted a race of slaves—conquered Gauls who had lost their liberty—and, as a debased population, had no right to political self-determination. This characterization drew on an older tradition, developed in the Middle Ages, that justified serfdom by a variety of intellectual constructs that reduced peasants to an inherited, almost subhuman status.[5] The aristocracy, by contrast, was not of Gallic descent. Rather, they were the descendants of the Franks, that is, the "free" warriors who had entered Gaul, defeated and expelled the Roman lords, and established their rights to rule. Such claims drew on the image presented by the first-century Roman historian Cornelius Tacitus, who glorified the free Germans in contrast to Romans of his day. Such claims also demanded a particular reading of the works of Gregory of Tours and other early medieval sources to emphasize the free, Germanic identity of the *nation française.*

Who actually held this right to rule—the aristocracy, as a collectivity, or the king—was a primary point of debate. In 1588 the royal propagandist Gui de Coquille went so far as to argue that Hugh Capet, founder of the royal lineage from which all subsequent French kings descended, had been of Saxon stock. This Saxon Germanic background made his royal successor a true Frenchman, a *vrai François.*[6] In the eighteenth century, aristocrats such as Louis de Saint-Simon, François de Salignac de Fénelon, and Henri de Boulainvilliers, agreed that the population of Gaul in Late Antiquity was essentially a race of slaves. In the fifth century, free Frankish warriors had acquired Gaul by right of conquest. They alone, and their descendants—the nobility—were the true French. The king should share power with them, as had been the case in the days of Charlemagne.

An analogous tradition developed in Poland, where elites attempted to deny that they were of Slavic origin altogether. As early as the mid-sixteenth century, Polish chroniclers had claimed that the Polish elite should be identified not with the masses of Slavic peasants who worked the lands but with the Sarmatians, an ancient steppe people mentioned by Greek and Roman ethnographers.[7] By the seventeenth century, the Sarmatian origins thesis had become a vehicle by which the elite *szlachta* differentiated themselves ethnically from their social inferiors.[8]

Revolutionary Nationalism

The French Revolution changed everything and nothing in this vision of the past. Particularly in France, the popular propaganda of the revolutionary period accepted this bipartite schema of Franks and Gauls, but reversed the values derived from it. In his influential pamphlet on the third estate, the French revolutionary theorist Abbé Sieyès accepted the Germanic origin of the nobility, but argued that this made them a foreign, conquering element in France. The true French people, descendants of the Gauls, had long borne the yoke of foreign servitude, first under the Romans and then under the Franks. It was time to send this alien race back to the forests of Franconia and return France to the third estate, the one true nation.

However, this nationalist claim ran counter to official revolutionary ideology that, while proclaiming the independence and sovereignty of each people, denied that a "people" could be defined by language, ethnicity, or origins. Rather, a willingness to support the common good against particular interests, to accept the liberties and laws of the Republic, were all that should be re-

21

quired.[9] Nevertheless, on a more practical level, the implicit assumption persisted that a shared cultural tradition, particularly embodied in the French language, defined the French nation.

The precursors to German nationalism, Johann Gottfried Herder and the Göttingen historians, also drew on the Tacitean myth, but initially within the context of a linguistic, cultural unity, which neither presupposed nor demanded political unity. Since the rediscovery of Tacitus's *Germania* at the end of the fifteenth century, humanists had become fascinated with the image of a free, pure Germanic people. From Conrad Celtis's *Germania illustrata* (1491) to Jacob Wimpleling's *Epitome rerum Germanicarum,* to Heinrich Bebel's *Proverbia Germanica,* and beyond, authors sought a German unity and history. However, this unity remained purely cultural, not political. German-speaking regions had never been united in a single, culturally homogeneous kingdom. Even in the Middle Ages, the "Holy Roman Empire" had always included important Slavic and Romance regions. Moreover, the deep divisions caused by the Reformation and the disasters of the Thirty Years' War ensured that political and social unity would remain outside the sphere of this cultural perspective until the nineteenth century.[10]

Still, within this cultural nationalism emerged the characteristics that, when politicized, would become formidable tools of political mobilization. These included the belief that a German "nation" had existed as early as the first century, when Arminius defeated the Roman general Varus and destroyed his army in the Teutoburg Forest in 9 C.E. These cultural nationalists also exalted the German language, which they saw as the embodiment of German identity, and emphasized the importance of education as a means of continuing and intensifying the appreciation of this heritage.

Not that this belief in the existence of a German "nation" implied a political mission, especially not an expansive one. Nothing is stronger evidence of the lack of a political dimension in Herder's thought than the idea that not only Germany but, indeed, every nationality was entitled to its own development in concord with its own genius. His enthusiasm for the Slavs was perhaps even greater than his enthusiasm for the Germans, urging the Slavic world to replace the "declining Latin-German culture" with their own. The "nationalism" of Herder and the Göttingen circle remained one of culture, not of political action.

German political nationalism emerged haltingly during the Napoleonic era in response to the French defeats of Prussia and the occupation of the Rhineland. A major force behind the creation of a popular resistance to the French, which would eventually lead to a spirit of insurrection in the populace, was Freiherr vom Stein, the Prussian minister of State (1804–1808). He urged poets and writers to contribute to the image of a unified German nation once the French were ousted. The geographical outlines of this German nation were, of course, uncertain: The former Holy Roman Empire was only about 25 percent German-speaking. Prussia was a kingdom in which at least six languages, in addition to German, were used. These included Polish, Latvian, Lusitian, and Estonian, while much of the intelligensia spoke French. German-speaking regions were divided not only by politics but by dialectical differences, religion, and a history of animosity dating back to the Thirty Years' War. Moreover, even the king of Prussia was wary of any mass movement that would involve the people in an educational or political role.

Thus, avowals of cultural unity by authors such as Friedrich Gottlieb Klopstock, Herder, and Gotthold Ephraim Lessing initially found no political resonance: The German princes had no interest in political concert, and the middle-class public had no political interest or agenda. Varnhagen von Ense, an educated upper-class Prussian, recalled no patriotic concern on watching the king depart Berlin in 1806 after his disastrous loss to Napoleon in the battle of Jena. He and others of his background felt sorry for him, but "were simply unable to muster any genuine political zeal that might include an exclusive preoccupation with political reports and communiqués all day long."[11] On the contrary, many German intellectuals with political interests were liberals and greeted Napoleon's victories with optimism.

What support there was for a politicization of Herder's cultural ideals came neither from the mainstream of the German intellectual world nor from the Prussian king but from the British, who sought to generate popular opposition to the French in the East that would continue to pressure Napoleon. The British hoped to open a "second Vendée"—an internal guerrilla resistance movement similar to that pursued by royalists in that stubborn region of France—by supporting insurrectionists in Prussia. This British goal coincided with that of Freiherr vom Stein, who was convinced that the Junker class was incapable of saving Prussia and sought to develop a sense of patriotism among the educated and cultural elites of the kingdom in order to create a more effective resistance to the French. This end was to be accomplished through a mobilization of the elements of earlier generations of cultural nationalist feeling: an emphasis on common language (rather than a common religious or political tradition, both of which were entirely lacking); a program of national education; and an emphasis on the place of the citizen as the link between the past and future of the nation.[12] Stein's interests thus dovetailed with those of the British, who funded intellectuals willing to combine culture and politics.

Chief among these German intellectuals was Johann Gottlieb Fichte, who was eager to politicize Germanic culture and did so by equating the Romans of the first century with the French of his day, and the Germanic resistors to Roman expansion with himself and his German contemporaries. The touchstone for a unified German identity thus became the descriptions of the German virtues in Tacitus's *Germania* and the account of Arminius and his destruction of Varus and his legion in Tacitus's *Annales*. This was a means of finding a German unity preceding the political complexities of the Holy Roman Empire and of showing how, in the past, Germans had resisted a Romance-speaking invader. As developed by Fichte in his *Addresses to the German Nation,* a unique German identity contrasted, on the one hand, with the Slavs, who "do not seem as yet to have developed distinctly enough in comparison with the rest of Europe to make it possible to give a definite description of them," and, on the other, with Romanized peoples of "Teutonic descent,"[13] that is, with the French. In contrast to each of these, the central virtue of German identity rested on its continuity in geography and its language. The relationship between language and identity was certainly nothing new in the nineteenth century.[14] More than half a century earlier, the French philosopher Étienne Bonnot de Condillac had argued that "each language expresses the character of the people who speak it."[15] Fichte, however, developed this tradition in very specific and provocative ways. As he stated in his Fourth Address, the Germans alone among the "neo-Europeans" remained in the original dwelling place of their ancestral stock and retained their original language.[16] It was this language, in particular, that united the German people and put them in direct contact with God's creation in a way that peoples such as the French, who had adopted Latinized language, could not hope to achieve. The reason was that, unlike Romance languages that built words from Latin and Greek roots, themselves formed in distant regions, German derived entirely from Germanic elements, originally coined to describe the world still inhabited by Germans. This language, therefore, was immediately transparent and comprehensible to all German speakers, placing them in immediate relationship with their environment and with each other.

Fichte's *Addresses* must certainly be understood within their immediate context: They might be termed "survivalist texts," intended to give hope and foster resistance in the immediate context of a French occupation, an occupation that was widely expected to last for many years. The rapid destruction of the French Empire ended the specific need for such sentiments, but their afterlife proved of enormous consequence.

The involvement of intellectuals such as Fichte in the cause of politics may not have had much influence on the outcome of the Napoleonic wars, but it connected them to the world of politics and action in a new way. While involving them in the sphere of political action, it brought them new prominence, financial rewards, and official patronage. This potent combination did not end with the Congress of Vienna, assembled in 1815 to restore Europe after Napoleon. Stein, who had taken the leadership role in recruiting intellectuals during the war, strengthened the connection between scholars and politicians in search of a unified Germany. In 1819 he founded the "Society for Older German Historical Knowledge (*Gesellschaft für ältere deutsche Geschichtskunde*)," whose motto, *Sanctus amor patriae dat animum* (The holy love of the Fatherland gives spirit), summarized a program rather than a truism. The *Gesellschaft* was a private organization, founded in consultation with such noted intellectuals as Goethe; Wilhelm von Humboldt; the Grimm brothers, Friedrich Carl von Savigny, and Karl Friedrich Eichhorn. Contributions from various German states and the German Bund financed the *Gesellschaft,* which dedicated itself to editing and publishing the *Monumenta Germaniae Historica* or the Historical Monuments of Germany. Initially, these contributions were hard to come by; the German states were not eager to contribute, and Stein was inclined to reject, for patriotic reasons, contributions from foreigners such as the Russian czar. Only gradually, as politicians realized that patriotic history could counterbalance revolutionary ideology, did Stein find the funding he needed to continue his project.

However, funding was only one problem. The other was determining just what the historical monuments of Germany were.

These were discovered according to the principles of scientific, Indo-European philology, which were being developed by classical philologists in the Netherlands and, more recently, in Göttingen.

Comparative Indo-European (or *Indogermanisch*) philology was born in 1786 when the English orientalist Sir William Jones recognized that Sanskrit, Greek, and Latin had sprung from a common source and that Gothic, Celtic, and old Persian were probably members of the same family.[17] Twenty-two years later, the German philologist Friedrich von Schlegel developed Jones's insight, although he argued in his *On the Language and Wisdom of the Indians (Über die Sprache und Weisheit der Inder),* that Sanskrit was the parent language of Greek, Latin, Persian, and the Germanic languages. In the following generation, the German scholars Franz Bopp and Jacob Grimm, as well as the Dane Rasmus Rask, took these early and rather intuitive suggestions, corrected them, elaborated a method for examining language development and affinity, and created the new science of Indo-European philology.[18] This rapidly developing new discipline made possible not only the organization and classification of the language family from which descended Slavic, Germanic, Hellenic, and Romance languages, but also the scientific study of the earliest forms of these languages. Since the Renaissance, German humanists had been fascinated by the resemblances among contemporary Germanic languages. They had marveled at the relationship between ancient languages, such as the Gothic Bible translated by the missionary Bishop Ulfilas in the fourth century, and the community of "Crimean Goths," allegedly still speaking a recognizably Germanic language into the sixteenth century. However, now it became possible to organize the knowledge of European languages into an interrelated and historically nuanced discipline. Philology—both the traditional classical tradition focusing on Greek and Latin texts, and the newer Germanic philology—lay at the heart of the methodological impulse of the new, scientific undertaking of the *Monumenta.*

The agenda of Stein's *Gesellschaft* was more than simply editing and publishing the sources of German history in the *Monumenta Germaniae Historica*. Before the sources could be edited, one had to establish a canon of those records of the past that were indeed sources of German history. This meant defining Germany in the past and laying claim to this past as inherently German. The scholars who undertook this task were not radical political nationalists. Nevertheless, their work fueled nationalist claims of extraordinary breadth. These editors claimed as these monuments all texts written in or about regions in which Germanic-speaking peoples had settled or ruled. First, the *Monumenta* editors claimed all those regions that had been part of the "Holy Roman Empire of the German Nation," from the south of Italy to the Baltic. In addition, they annexed the whole of Frankish history, including the chronicles and acts of Merovingian and Carolingian kings in the regions of Gaul that are today France and Belgium. They absorbed the laws of the Visigoths, the Burgundians, and the Lombards, Germanic-speaking groups that had settled into what is today Italy and the Rhone valley. They appropriated the county of Flanders and all of the Netherlands east of the Schelde because these areas were settled by the Germanic-speaking Frisians. By deciding to publish the works of a series of ancient authors, they swallowed up Africans, such as Victor Vitensis, who wrote on the Germanic Vandals in Africa; Gallo-Romans like Ausonius; and Roman senators, such as Cassidorius and Symmachus. The result of the *Monumenta* perspective was to define Germany in a much more sweeping manner than even the *Lied der Deutschen,* with its infamous lines "From the Meuse to the Memel, from the Etsch to the Belt (*Von der Maas bis an die Memel/ Von der Etsch bis an den Belt*)," had ever dared.

By defining the corpus of what was German history, the *Monumenta* set the parameters within which Germany would search for its past. The Goths, the Franks, the Burgundians, the Vandals, and other early "peoples" were identified by an uninterrupted history, which preceded the establishment of the medieval Holy Roman Empire and which reached through the nineteenth century.

Philology and Nationalism

The presumed criteria for the inclusion of these "peoples" in the *Historical Monuments of Germany* were that they were "Germanic," that is, that they belonged to the same linguistic family as did the Germans of the nineteenth century. If the texts published by the *Monumenta* created the object, philology created the method. This was true in two senses. First, Indo-European philology gave new "objective" criteria to peoplehood along the lines of Herder and Fichte's mystical linguistics. Second, philology, already developed as the essential tool of classical studies, became the primary tool of medieval historical study, a tool that it used to discover the prehistory of German nationalism.

These twin tools of German nationalism—texts and philological analysis—not only created *German* history, but, by implication, *all* history. They were a readily exportable package, easily applied to any corpus of texts in any language. Moreover, since German standards of "scientific" historical scholarship increasingly dominated nineteenth-century universities in Europe and even America, foreign historians trained in the German seminar method and text-critical scholarship served as ambassadors of nationalistic analysis when they returned to their own countries. Earlier, Herder-type movements, such as pan-Slavism, were quickly politicized, and nations and would-be nations all followed suit with their own apparatus of national self-creation. These included a corpus of "monuments of national history" and philologists (many German educated) to elucidate the ancient origins of their nations. Historical scholarship and nationalism became one.

The French reaction to the politicization of German scholarship, late and defensive, followed the catastrophe of the Franco-Prussian war in 1870. Some, such as the philologist Léon Gautier, went so far as to attribute the German victory to their training as philologists: "The Prussian fights in the same way he criticizes a text, with the same precision and method."[19] The solution, obviously, was to imitate the German model, not only in creating university chairs of philology and history, of which some 250 were founded between 1876 and 1879,[20] but also by absorbing the philological method of the German tradition. Of course, the French attempted to purge it of its German, nationalist character, but sought to eliminate only the first adjective, not the second. Philology remained a tool of nationalism. In a manner reminiscent of Fichte, who insisted that only a natural language placed a people in proper relationship to the world, French philologists argued that the literary creations of medieval France were "indigenous plants, born spontaneously in the earth of the fatherland."[21] Thus, ironically, while the French search for "scientific" philology was an attempt to escape "Romanticism," "Romanticism" was understood as essentially "Germanness"; to this end, the French philologists appropriated the very tools of Germanic nationalism. The resulting philology, no less a glorification of a romanticized view of the Middle Ages, was also a glorification of the French self-myth of scientific exactitude. In the process, the republican sense of "citizen," independent of any historicized national language and culture, was discarded in favor of an ethnic nationalist one.

Across Europe, the pernicious effects of the philological method of identifying people by language were myriad.[22] First, the infinite gradations of broad linguistic groups in Europe were chopped up by scientific rules into separate languages. Since the spoken and written realities never corresponded exactly to these artificial rules, "official" forms—usually systematized versions of a local dialect, often of a politically powerful group or important city—were invented and imposed through state-sponsored educational systems. The result was that linguistic boundaries became much more rigid and whole traditions, oral and in some cases even written, virtually disappeared under the pressure of "standard" usage. What this amounted to was nothing less than the virtual invention of languages, including not only such obvious cases as Ukrainian, Bulgarian, Serbian, Croatian, Slovine, Latvian, Hebrew, Norwegian, Irish, Dutch, and Romanian, but, in more subtle ways, German and Italian as well. Not surprisingly, proponents of these "standard" languages tended initially to ascribe them to real or desired political boundaries. In few cases did all of the population of a given polity actually speak even the favored dialect of this language. Even in a country such as France, which had centuries-long traditions of political frontiers and where norms of proper usage had been developing for centuries, probably not much more than 50 percent of French men and women spoke French as their native language in 1900. Others spoke a variety of Romance languages and dialects, while in Brittany, Alsace, and Lorraine, Celtic and Germanic languages predominated. In other cases, the national language was spoken by a distinct minority, as in Norway, or populations used a variety of languages for different purposes and in varying combinations for trade, culture, politics, or domestic life.

Thus, everywhere, individuals, families, and communities found themselves isolated from the "national language" and under pressure to give up their traditions of speech. This could mean anything from simply adopting vocabulary, standard pronounciation, and modified systems of inflections, as in the case of the inhabitants of Holland, to abandoning dialects or ancient linguistic traditions such as Provençal in the south of France. Finally, it could mean learning, in state-supported and -mandated schools, a lan-

31

guage from a whole different linguistic family, as in the cases of the Britons and the Basques in France or the Romanians and the Slavs in Hungary.

As a result, ambitious national educational programs, including language instruction of the sort urged by Stein, became essential for the creation of a population capable of using the national language. Thus, educational institutions became the locus for the creation of the nation-state, both through the inculcation of nationalist ideology and, more subtly, through the dissemination of a national language in which this ideology was incarnate. Language became the vehicle for teaching the national history of the "people" whose language this was and whose political aspirations the language expressed. However, the new philology allowed nationalist educators and ideologues to go even further: It made possible the creation of a national, "scientific" history that projected both national language and national ideology into a distant past.

This projection was possible because the triumph of philology had a second and equally pernicious effect on the development of nationalism. Once national languages were established—in theory if not on the lips of the population—then the rules of Indo-European philology made it possible for linguists to ascribe ancient vernacular texts, some over a thousand years old, to these languages. The rules of linguistics made it possible for scholars to claim linear descent from these early texts to modern versions of national languages. Thus, linguists could speak of the ancient monuments of their nations: The oldest texts in "German" date from the eighth century; in "French," from the ninth; in "Slovine," from the eleventh century; "Armenian," from the sixth. But comparative philology made it possible to go further back still: Comparative study of different Indo-European language traditions made possible the elaboration of rules for the systematic changes in languages, allowing historical philologists to work backwards from extant versions of languages to hypothetical reconstructions of much more ancient languages from preliterate times. Thus, philologists provided nationalists with a means of projecting their nations into a distant, preliterate past. In the tradition of Fichte, they claimed that textual evidence, or lacking that, the historical philology, proved the existence of discrete "linguistic communities" sharing the same vision of life, the same social and religious values, the same political systems. The birth of peoples corresponded to the time when these separate, identifiable languages hived off from their common Germanic, Slavic, Romance, or Hellenic stock to form a linguistic and cultural unity.

A Dangerous Inheritance

This kind of language-based claim to cultural ethnicity has largely survived the discrediting of the more primitive forms of pseudo-historical nationalism. Even today, neonationalists acknowledge that the political self-consciousness of modern nationalism is a nineteenth- or twentieth-century phenomenon, yet attempt to claim that while *political* ethnicity is of recent vintage, *cultural* ethnicity is much more ancient. The people was a people, in other words, before it knew itself and language is both the sign and innermost reality of this immutable identity. Thus, journalists and international agencies reporting on so-called ethnic disturbances focus on language differences. When, for example, we are told that Lithuania is inhabited by "ethnic Lithuanians and Russians," what this actually means is that x percent of the population of that new state speak Lithuanian as a first language and y percent speak Russian. If, as in Brittany or Ireland, such claims can no longer be made because of the massive loss of indigenous language in the past century, then what is meant is that "x percent *should* speak a given language because their ancestors did."

Philologically based scientific history, drafted into the service of nationalism, led back ultimately to the period between the third

33

and eleventh centuries. The period between the disappearance of the Roman Empire and the formation of new communities from which modern nation-states and nationalist movements attempted to trace their legitimacy was also the period when new language groups became localizable within Europe. In this period, then, known as the moment of "primary acquisition," the ancestors of modern nations—speaking their national language, which carried and expressed specific cultural and intellectual modes—first appeared in Europe, conquering once and for all their sacred and immutable territories and, in so doing, acquiring once and for all their natural enemies. Maps and studies of the Migration Period (or, in Romance-speaking countries, the Invasion Period) showed, in dense jumbles of lines and arrows, the appearance both within and outside of the Empire of peoples distinguished by language or dialect, custom, dress, and religion.

Ethnoarchaeology

With linguistic tools to track down peoples before they knew they were peoples, it was not long before another "scientific" discipline began to be employed to the same end. This was ethnoarchaeology. Once one could determine linguistically the location of a "people," then it was up to archaeologists to find the physical evidence of the cultural specificities of that people. Surely if language corresponded to a specific people who shared common customs and values, these same cultural differences would be manifest in the physical artifacts recoverable by archaeologists. This quest was pursued with particular zeal by German archaeologists, interested in the origins of the Germanic peoples, and, later, by Slavic archaeologists interested in the origins of the Slavs. The most important proponent of the thesis that specific traditions of material culture could be connected to linguistic groups was Gustaf Kos-

sinna, who set about establishing the direct correspondence between early peoples and distinct material cultures. He believed
himself capable of identifying ethnic groups—known first through
classical and medieval texts, then identified by philology—by a systematic investigation of archaeological materials, an investigation
that could trace peoples far beyond the historical period and into
the Iron Age. Such distinctive ethnic markers gave a physical dimension to the linguistic parameters of ethnicity. Thus Kossinna
posited a direct, one-to-one relationship between language, material culture, and peoples known from historical sources.[23] Most important, it made it possible for Kossinna and his followers to trace
the migration routes of early medieval peoples as they wandered
from their original homelands into the Roman world.[24]

The implications of this new tradition of ethnic archaeology
were particularly important in the development of nineteenth- and
twentieth-century territorial claims. In particular, it encouraged
modern states such as Germany to claim regions of neighboring
countries on the basis that these territories were the original homelands of the German peoples. Thus, the expansion of the German
crusading orders into the east in the thirteenth century, or of the
Third Reich in the twentieth, could be justified not as *conquest* but
simply as a *return*. More recently, similar archaeological arguments
have been used, for example, in conflicts between Hungarians and
Slovenes, Albanians and Serbs, and Estonians and Germans.

The Toxic Waste

The heritage of nationalist philology and archaeology continues to
weigh heavily on the map of European nations. They "scientifi-
cally" established the essential components of nationhood: language, territory, and distinct culture in an ancient past. Through
the new history and the new philology, many believed that com-

mon unity could be established, ancient injustices could be nurtured, and ancient claims vindicated.

The stories are familiar enough to any student of Western European history. Germanic peoples, such as the Burgundians, the Goths, or the Lombards, living in southern Scandinavia, began to migrate south, driven by climatic change, famine, overpopulation, or some as-yet-unknown compulsion. These peoples moved across the whole length of Europe, taking their languages, customs, and traditions with them and transmitting their unique identities to their children, through generations of migration, until they found themselves on the borders of the Roman Empire. There, led by their heroic warrior-kings, descendants of ancient royal or noble families, they successfully challenged Rome and carved out Germanic kingdoms from the remains of the Empire. These heroes included the Ostrogoth Theodoric, descended from the ancient royal family of the Amals; Alaric, the Visigothic leader of the Balth dynasty; Alboin, commander of the Lombards and a member of the Gauti; and the Frank Clovis, a member of the Merovingian royal family. Slightly later, similar commanders of Slavic peoples, such as the Croatian family of Chrobatos and Isperihk, commander of Bulgars, led their peoples into the ruins of the Empire. These events were argued to have been the moments of "primary acquisition," from which point began the history of the nations of Europe.

Today these events still offer the common basis for distinguishing the broad outlines of European ethnic groups. To be sure, not all these ethnic groups are still around, and even among those that are, not all are nation-states. Still, their leaders can aspire to nationhood and encourage their people to participate in the struggle for self-rule. The international community can offer no objections to these aspirations except for practicality, economic viability, or brute force—weak arguments in the face of deeply held convictions of the rights of peoples to self-determination.

But in spite of the emotional appeal of these historical and linguistic claims, nothing in the historical record justifies them. Congruence between early medieval and contemporary "peoples" is a myth. Linguistic and historical arguments break down quickly in contemporary issues of ethnic difference, and they are even less appropriate for distinguishing among the "peoples" of Europe in the early Middle Ages. In Northern Ireland, religion, not language, separates hostile parties. In the former Yugoslavia, Serbian and Croatian are dialects of the same language, one spoken by a traditionally Orthodox community, the other by a traditionally Roman Catholic one, although nationalist leadership in both actually comes from agnostic or atheistic political opportunists. Both in large, hegemonic states and in aspiring independence movements, claims that "we have always been a people" actually are appeals to *become* a people—appeals not grounded in history but, rather, attempts to create history. The past, as has often been said, is a foreign country, and we will never find ourselves there.

The Confusion of the Past

In Late Antiquity and the early Middle Ages, it is often hard to know just what languages differing "peoples" spoke; indeed, anecdotal evidence suggests that they often spoke a variety of languages. At the same time, ancient and medieval observers often indicated that groups that they identified as different peoples shared a common language. Nor does language necessarily correspond to other cultural traditions, such as forms of dress, jewelry, pottery, or weapons. The hypothetical prehistoric maps of the major language groups—Germanic, Slavic, Celtic, Baltic, Romance, and the like—do not correspond to any specific differences in material culture that can be identified archaeologically. The simplistic maps of material cultures, elaborated by Kossinna and his followers, have

37

proved to be mythic: One by one the "distinguishing" characteristics of ethnic material culture have been shown to be much more or much less widely distributed than the patterns suggested by language. As the British historian Chris Wickham has remarked, "a man or woman with a Lombard-style brooch is no more necessarily a Lombard than a family in Bradford with a Toyota is Japanese; artifacts are no secure guide to ethnicity."[25]

Language apparently neither corresponded to nor determined culture. Political elites throughout history often have spoken languages quite different from those of their subordinates. Moreover, part of the conceptual problem of understanding the peoples of Europe in the early Middle Ages is that, following the model of nineteenth-century ethnic nationalism, historians are inclined to think geographically: They look for a correspondence between territories, regions, or kingdoms, and ethnic groups who occupied them. Just as in the case of modern, complex societies, however, the boundaries separating "peoples" in the early Middle Ages were usually not geographical but political, economic, or social. Moreover, where geographic distinctions did exist, these were *within* areas, not *between* areas.

The populations of towns in Gaul, Spain, Italy, and the Balkans were distinct from the populations in the surrounding countryside. Townspeople comprised military officers and government officials from across the Empire, merchants from Syria and Asia Minor, and Jews who had lived for generations in these outposts of Mediterranean society. In the sixth century, Paris, for example, had a series of bishops whose names suggest their origins from the eastern Mediterranean, an indication that control of this central religious institution may have been in the hands of the Syrian and Greek communities. At the same time, indigenous aristocrats continued to dominate the countryside. The arrival of Goths, Burgundians, and Franks did little to change this situation. Archaeological evidence had shown that the barbarians, like the governors and military commanders they replaced, settled primarily in towns where they could maintain political control through unity, while they lived on the revenues collected from the estates assigned to them. Outside the towns, barbarian forces limited their actual settlements to strategic military sites.

Later barbarian settlements reversed this pattern. In the Balkans, cities—particularly those along the coast, such as Zadar, Trogir, Split, Dubrovnik, Budva, and Kotor—remained Greek-speaking outposts of Roman culture. The surrounding rural population was dominated by a steppe confederation, known as the Avars, which eventually merged into Slavic societies. German expansion into northeastern Europe likewise created cities that had little in common—culturally, politically, or linguistically—with the surrounding countryside they controlled.

These medieval patterns were long lasting. Well into the twentieth century, important cities, such as those in the Baltics, remained culturally, linguistically, and politically distinct from the surrounding countryside without creating "national" tensions. On the other hand, language that might, at first glance, be understood in terms of ethnic difference often simply implied social or political distinction. In the nineteenth century, when Estonian peasants referred to *saks* (Saxons), the word meant primarily "lord" or "master" not "German" in some ethnic, linguistic, nationalistic sense.[26] Over the long term, peoples simply do not map geographically.

Only the horrors of the twentieth century have created the illusion that language and ethnicity could or should be mapable. Suppression of cultural diversity in states such as Spain, France, and Turkey made Basques, Catalans, Britons, Armenians, Kurds, and other minorities "disappear" from nation-states. The Holocaust and the "ethnic cleansing" of Eastern Europe that followed World War II drove thousands of German-speaking inhabitants of Eastern Europe west, and made the populations of cities such as Danzig, Königsberg, Riga, and Vilna largely the same as the surrounding rural populations for the first time in their histories. However, there are signs that the older pattern of stratified linguistic and cultural diversity is re-emerging. This is particularly evident in the great cities of Europe, where linguistic and cultural stratification once more characterizes both ends of the population's spectrum. At the top, major multinational corporations and scientific institutions operate largely or entirely in English with little regard for local language traditions. At the lower end of the social scale, these cities have experienced substantial growth in the numbers of people who trace their origins to Turkey, North Africa, the Indian subcontinent, and other parts of Asia. These immigrants live their lives speaking Arabic, Turkish, and other languages distant from those spoken by the middle class. These developments, which are greeted by hostility and fear as novel occurrences, are actually a return to a much more ancient pattern of ethnic diversity. Europe is indeed beginning once more to resemble its past.

Thus, after almost two centuries of attempts to map ethnicity linguistically, archaeologically, and historically, one must conclude that all of these programs have failed. The fundamental reason is that ethnicity exists first and last in people's minds. Yet ethnicity's locus in people's minds does not make it ephemeral; on the contrary, it is all the more real and powerful as a result. A creation of the human will, it is impervious to mere rational disproof.

And yet, in fairness to nineteenth- and twentieth-century scientific nationalists, the categories of nationhood they developed did not spring from a void: They drew on a much more ancient tradition of identifying peoples, a tradition already developed in the very historical sources that historians and philologists attempted to use to find peoples in the past. In many significant ways, nineteenth-century ethnography was but a continuation, with more refined tools, of the ethnographic tradition of Classical Antiquity.

Chapter Two

Imagining Peoples in Antiquity

It is all very well to point out, as we did in Chapter 1, that ethnic nationalism is of recent origin. It would be more accurate to say that the particular type of ethnic nationalism that we know today is of recent origin. In past ages, people had different but equally powerful ways of identifying themselves, distinguishing themselves from others, and mobilizing these identities for political purposes. However, we often have difficulty recognizing the differences between these earlier ways of perceiving group identities and more contemporary attitudes because, again, we are trapped in the very historical process we are attempting to study. Already we have used the terms "people," "ethnicity," "race," and "ethnogenesis," as though these words carried some sort of objective, fixed meaning. While the particular way that we use them is novel, these words and their equivalents have a long history reaching back at least to the fifth century B.C.E. They are inherited from several millennia of discussions, observations, and assumptions and thus come to us burdened with the cultural baggage of the past. Long before Fichte or Herder, these terms were important and resonant elements in the Western European intellectual tradition.

It's no use trying to invent new terms for past social groups: We are stuck with the vocabulary we have inherited. However, we do need to understand the historical process that has given them meaning through the ages. The categories by which Europeans attempt to understand the differences among social groups are inherited from both Classical and biblical Antiquity. Briefly stated, there were two sorts of "peoples." The one was *constitutional*, based on law, allegiance, and created by a historical process. The other, standing largely outside the process of historical change was *biological*, based on descent, custom, and geography. Crudely, one can characterize the difference as "us" and "them"; "civilized" and "barbarian." (The tradition lives on today: In many places in Europe and America, historical museums deal only with "us" while museums of natural history contain, along with displays of animals, plants, and minerals, native Americans, Africans, and other "natural peoples.") When, in the third and fourth centuries, authors first started to describe the new "peoples" who would become the Europeans of today, they drew on these deeply held traditions. Thus, we need to understand the influence of assumptions derived both from Greco-Roman Antiquity and from the Bible on those authors who are our only sources for the new societies that appear in Europe at the end of the ancient world.

Thus, in order to see beneath these layers of cultural accretions, we must first explore the origins of our language, of ethnicity, of peoplehood. We must see how literary traditions, power politics, religious faith, and imperialism in Antiquity changed and molded the ways that ethnographers perceived and described human society.

Natural Peoples and the Roman People

The origins of European ethnographical reflection start at least with the so-called "Histories" of Herodotus of Halicarnassos, written around the middle of the fifth century. Herodotus was the first ethnographer, and his way of understanding and describing the world remains with us today.

Herodotus invented both history and ethnography as he wrote about the origins of the wars between the Greeks and the Persians. Not content to be either a "battle historian" or a political historian, he conceived of the conflict between the Greeks and the Persians as but a phase in a very long process that brought Europe and Asia into deadly collision. Thus, his inquiries were not limited to the political and military events of the Persian War. Instead, he drew on what he had seen, heard, and read in his travels throughout the eastern Mediterranean and Asia Minor to present what today would be called a "total history" of the known world. The units of this world were peoples (*ethne;* sing., *ethnos*), themselves often subdivided into tribes (*gene;* sing., *genos*), whose religious traditions, social customs, language, material culture, and economic systems he described in elaborate detail.

In general, according to Herodotus, peoples are differentiated geographically and culturally. While Herodotus recognized that peoples might migrate from one region to another, in his histories a specific people normally inhabits a specific geographical area to which it gives its name. Egypt is the territory inhabited by the Egyptians, just as Cilicia is the country occupied by Cilicians or Assyria by Assyrians.[1] Herodotus tells the story that Aristagoras, the ruler of Miletus, had a bronze map showing the countries of the Lydians, Phrygians, Cappadocians or Syrians, Cilicians, Armenians, Matieni, and Cissia.[2] Most peoples have their own language, that of the Phrygians being the most ancient, although not every people speaks a different language. Finally, peoples have their own religions and customs, among which Herodotus finds most significant those defining the spheres of activities of women, burial practices, and economic activities.

The distinctions between *ethne* (peoples) and *gene* (tribes) are fluid, but Herodotus does not see any problem in identifying

43

major and minor groups, differentiated by further refinements in cultural traits. The categories appear to him objective and self-evident. Likewise, he seldom pauses to discuss why he knows that a particular tribe belongs to one or another *ethnos,* even if members may not always admit their membership. In discussing the Ionians, for example, whom he characterizes as the weakest of the Hellenic peoples, he states that, out of shame, most mainland descendants of Ionians refuse to acknowledge their Ionian origins.[3]

Although Herodotus accepts the objective existence of peoples, he is aware that they can both come into being and disappear. About the origins of peoples, he willingly tells both indigenous myths of the origins of different *ethne* as well as Greek legends that connect them with Hercules, Minos, or some other figure from Greek mythology. The legends of ethnogenesis, or people formation, which he tells, are essentially of two sorts. One is the account of the origins of the royal or leading family, usually told in terms of a mythical genealogy that establishes the enduring character of that family and its right to authority over the people. In his detailed discussion of the Scyths, he provides two alternative genealogical accounts of this, the most recent of peoples. The first, which he says is how the Scyths themselves describe their origin, states that they descended from the three sons of Targitaos: Lipoxais, Arpoxais, and Colaxais. The Auchates Scyths descend from the first; the Catiares and Traspies from the second, and the Paralatae from the third. Following this indigenous myth, he reports an account told by Pontic Greeks that attached the origins of the Scythian kings to the Greek hero Hercules.[4] Herodotus himself favors neither of the origin myths. He prefers to avoid the question altogether, arguing that the Scyths arrived in the Pontic region having been chased from their homeland in Asia by the Massagetae.

Besides describing the origins of peoples as though they were all descended from a common ancestor, Herodotus also occasionally reports ethnogenesis through splintering and intermarriage, phenomena no doubt familiar to Greek colonists, but projected onto non-Greeks as well. Thus, the Lycians were the descendants of Cretans expelled with their leader Sarpedon by his brother Minos. The Sauromatae spring from Scythian youths who seduced and married Amazons.[5] The disappearance of peoples is more unusual, although Herodotus recognizes that peoples of his day sometimes occupied regions inhabited in former times by others who may have left traces of their language in topographical names. The Cimmerians, driven into Asia from their homeland by the Scyths, were later expelled from Asia by the Lydians, leaving only some place names as evidence of their passage.

Thus, Herodotus has a broad and nonjudgmental sense of how peoples came into being and disappeared. Whether descendants from a common ancestor or new offshoots of a prior people, whether absorbed into others or vanished from their original homelands, peoples can come into existence, flourish, and disappear as a result of the passage of time.

Just as geographical area and language are important but not absolutely defining for each *ethnos,* Herodotus also assumes some form of political system. Each *ethnos* or *genos* has its king or rulers. However, political forms do not play a major role in Herodotus's discussions of peoples. Moreover, the loss of political independence does not mean the destruction of a people: The Medes and later the Persians could conquer Asia without affecting the status of the peoples who inhabited it. In part, this was the result of the Persian system of government, which generally sought not to destroy local elites or political institutions, but to coopt them. Thus, even within larger political entities, peoples maintain their identities and personalities. While freedom may be a characteristic of some peoples, abject servitude may characterize others.

Although physical characteristics may be part of Herodotus's description of peoples, these tend to be more the result of geography than heredity. In spite of the biological metaphors implicit in the language of *genos* and *ethnos,* Herodotus does not assume what would later be considered racial or biological differences among the known peoples. If Ethiopians and Indians have black semen, if Northern peoples are tall and fair, the reason is the proximity or distance from the equator, not the result of inherited traits.

Herodotus's Heirs

Herodotus's panoramic description of peoples became the basis for all subsequent European ethnology. His categories, his attempts to classify, his stereotypes are still with us. However, many geographers and historians were far from happy with many of his most basic assumptions. In spite of (or perhaps even because of) his enormous influence, Herodotus was commonly seen by later ancients as "the Father of Lies."

First, later Greeks and Romans were disturbed by his essentially value-neutral approach to the customs and peoples he observed. Himself from an Ionian city in Asia Minor, whose population was by no means purely Greek in custom or language, Herodotus refused to pass judgments concerning the traditions and cultures he observed. This openness, shared by other pre-Socratic Ionians, may be a characteristic of otherwise lost Persian historiography to which, Herodotus, born into a Greek-speaking family in the Persian Empire, is indebted.[6] He certainly describes the Persians as "of all men those who most welcome foreign custom."[7] He recounts with apparent approval how Darius was said to have asked Greeks at his court if they would be willing to eat the corpses of their fathers, and when they replied in horror that they would never do so, he summoned to their presence Indians who did eat their parents' dead bodies. He asked them if they would be willing to burn their parents' corpses, a suggestion they rejected with equal horror.[8] For Herodotus, the traditions of the Scyths, the Greeks, the Egyptians, and the Persians were all of equal value. Every people, he observed, would no doubt find their own customs the most excellent, and he did nothing to dispute such a perspective.

Perhaps equally important in understanding Herodotus's neutral appreciation of cultures was his own political situation. Unlike later historians and ethnographers, he had no direct political relationship either with the Persians or the Greek cities that opposed them. Although he had traveled extensively and lived a considerable time in Athens, he remained an outsider with no fixed position in the power relationships that increasingly defined Greek and Persian perspectives. Such was emphatically not the case with later authors, particularly after the conquests of Alexander the Great. Thereafter, Greek authors would be part of an imperialist cultural tradition. Their interest in the "other" would be intimately connected with a concern for dominance, a perspective naturally inherited by Roman imperialist authors.

Thus, Herodotus represents a cultural perspective that might be termed "pre-Orientalist" in the sense developed by the American literary critic Edward W. Said as "an ontological and epistemological distinction made between 'the Orient' and (most of the time) 'the Occident.'"[9] This refusal to denigrate the customs of others earned him the epithet of "philobarbarian" from later writers who dismissed everyone who was not Greek-speaking as inferior ("barbarian" originally meant one who speaks gibberish). At the same time, these same critics used his material to attempt to prove the excellence of Greco-Roman tradition over all others, especially those of the "East." There is great irony in this almost constant stream of denigration since, as one scholar pointed out, "Herodotus had described, briefly or at length, some fifty or more peoples. Five to eight hundred years later, Pliny, Solinus, and Mela referred to thirty-four of the same peoples, and in terms that are either identical with or very similar to those used by the Greek historian."[10]

Besides objecting to his pro-"barbarian" attitudes, the second objection of subsequent writers to Herodotus's work was to the manner in which he used the characteristics with which he described peoples. Each people had its complex of traits, including customs, origins, region, and political form, but while these traits served to identify and distinguish them from their neighbors, they did not constitute the peoples as such. Later authors, such as the Roman polymath Pliny the Elder, turned this system on its head. These traits, along with geographical boundaries, became the determining factors in ethnic identity, not simply characteristics of those belonging to a particular group. Herodotus, for example, had been careful to distinguish between the various Scyths and their non-Scythian neighbors. The Neuri share Scythian customs and beliefs but Herodotus did not consider them Scyths, presumably because they had a different self-perception. The Melanchlaeni differ only from the Scyths in that they wear black cloaks, but they, too, are somehow not Scythian.

For Pliny and other Romans, who preferred order to ambiguity (and perhaps accuracy), such confusing categorizations would not do. Pliny wanted peoples to be clearly distinguishable, and he was particularly eager to classify them by where they lived. Thus all the *gentes* (the Latin equivalent of *gene*) living beyond the Danube are Scythians, regardless of what they might have considered themselves. These included the Getae, called by the Romans Dacians; the Sarmatae, Aorsi, Base-born Scythians (*Scythae degeneres*), Alani, Rhoxolani, and Sarmatian Iazyges.[11] The fourth-century Roman historian Ammianus Marcellinus is even more sweeping, stating that the *gentes* of the Scythians are innumerable and stretch to no known limit.[12] He identifies both Asian and European Scythian peoples, who stretch east to China and southeast to the Ganges.[13] Such territorialization and classification, typical of Roman concerns for precision and order, objectified and externalized the identity of *gentes* in a way entirely foreign to Herodotus.

The third objection to Herodotus posed by most later ethnographers was his sense of historical change, of ethnogenesis. Geographers and encyclopedists, in particular, described peoples in an eternal present, reducing or eliminating even the mythic elements of Herodotus's processual approach to peoples. Pliny, for example, delighted in combining as many sources as possible, including peoples long disappeared, with contemporary ethnic groups in his *Natural History.* The result was a sort of law of conservation of peoples—no people ever disappeared, no trait ever changed. At best, an old people might acquire a new name and novel, even contradictory, customs and characteristics, but the perceptive Roman could still recognize them for what they were. Such people were, in a sense, more a part of the natural world than the historical world. Moreover, the geographical location of peoples took on increasing importance as Roman contact with barbarians increased. The maps of the Roman world were crowded, as these compilers sought to fill their land masses with as many peoples as possible.

Gentes and the Populus

The characteristics of custom, geographical location, and permanence led to subtle but important differences in the way that subsequent Roman historians and ethnographers described social groups. First, they described themselves and others according to fundamentally different characteristics. Romans alone were given a sense of historical development, fluidity, and complexity. The ethnogenesis of the Roman people, as enshrined in works of Virgil and Livy, created a *populus* out of disparate *gentes.* For Livy, Roman identity was the result of a continuous process of political amalgamation. First, Aneas united the Trojans and the Aborigines "under one law and one name."[14] Likewise, Romulus called together the "multitude" and gave them laws by which they could co-

49

alesce into a single body of people.[15] Thus, the *populus Romanus* alone, unlike foreign "peoples," had a history. That history was the story of how the Roman people, as a body of individuals who lived according to a single law, came into being. Here was no question of putative unity of ancestry, geography, culture, language, or tradition. Throughout its long history, membership in the *populus Romanus* was a question of constitutional law, not natural law, and, thus, theoretically accessible to all.

The constitutional nature of the Roman people is reminiscent of Herodotus's understanding of the process by which some barbarian peoples were formed and transformed. Not so for Roman observers, such as Pliny or Ammianus Marcellinus. For them, the Romans were utterly different from other peoples, whose fixed identities were drawn not from association and acceptance of a political and legal system but, rather, from geographical, cultural, and linguistic criteria. Whether the terms employed were *populus, gens, natio,* or *tribus,* Romans categorized their neighbors, enemies, and subjects according to a system that imputed objective and immutable criteria. Thus, other "peoples" had no history, since their origins were lost in the time of myth, and membership was determined by birth, not by choice. They only became part of history when they entered the sphere of Roman existence.

The only Roman author to adopt, at least in part, Herodotus's more neutral vision of the "other" was Cornelius Tacitus. Both in his *Agricola,* in which he depicts the inhabitants of Britain, and especially in his *Germania,* an account of the inhabitants of Europe beyond the Rhine, he demonstrates a sympathy for these peoples otherwise lacking in classical ethnography. And yet—even in his presentations of the Britons, to whom he ascribes the most noble condemnation of Roman imperialism, and in his description of the Germans, the most detailed ethnographic presentation since Herodotus on the Scyths—Tacitus cannot fully escape the ethnographic tradition that constructs non-Romans as the "other."

He characterizes the Britons as more virtuous than the Gauls, since, unlike the former, they had not yet lost their courage along with their freedom. He praised their noble desire for vengeance against those who had enslaved them. He places in the mouth of their leader Calgacus the characterization of Roman policy as simply: "They create a desert and call it a peace."[16] And yet numerous details of his moving descriptions of the Britons show that he really did not know much about them and reverted to many of the old stereotypes of other, less positively inclined Roman authors. To the Caledonians he erroneously ascribes Germanic origin because of their red hair and large limbs. The Southern Silures, because of their dark complexion and curly hair, he assumes migrated from Spain. He is better informed about those of southeast Briton, whom he recognizes to be close to the Gauls in language, religion, and customs. However, beyond these very general and largely external divisions, he has little to say about specific customs, organizations, and traditions of the various *gentes*. Tacitus describes their religion as *superstitio*. Their characteristics, such as ferocity, and their distinctive military tactics are less individualized descriptions than commonplaces of barbarian custom.[17] Their nobility, courage, and love of freedom are more a device for Tacitus to condemn the Emperors Nero and Domitian, whom he hated, than a reflection of a genuine understanding of the Britons themselves.

Although more detailed and informed, Tacitus's description of the Germans is also within the broad tradition of post-Herodotian classical ethnography. His vocabulary does not differentiate between large populations and their smaller components, all of which he terms *gentes*. However, he is sensitive and accurate in his descriptions of the rise and fall of different "peoples," the distinction between large groups such as the Suebi and their various individual *gentes,* and the varying cultural and political traditions within these peoples. Still, the received ethnographic tradition is ever present. Consider the account of the origin of the Germans

51

from the three sons of Mannus, followed by an account of Hercules's travels. Tacitus's avowed skepticism of both legends, followed by his own opinion on the origins of the Germans, strongly echoes Herodotus's account of the origins of the Scyths and may be derived from Posidonius, a Hellenistic historian of the first century B.C.E. Elsewhere in Tacitus's description of the Germans, one hears echoes of Julius Caesar, Livy, and Pliny. Just as with the Britons in his *Agricola,* in his *Germania,* Tacitus finds much to praise in the Germans, especially those largely uncorrupted by Roman vices. However, here, too, he is fully within the post-Herodotean ethnographic tradition of making value judgments on the customs of the barbarians. If Tacitus finds much to praise rather than to blame, he is still far removed from Herodotus's belief in the essential equality of the customs of peoples.

If Tacitus came closer than other Roman authors to a nuanced description of non-Romans, his work had little effect on subsequent writers. Until the end of the Roman world and, indeed, far beyond, historians continued to view the world neatly divided into the Romans and barbarians, "us" and "them."[18]

The Gentiles and the People of God

The Roman dichotomous world was not unique. The Jews shared a parallel sense of social categorization into the people of God, *am,* and the other peoples, the *goyim* or, as they are commonly termed from the Latin translation for "peoples," the gentiles. The Bible presents two models of peoples. The first, implied in translated terms such as *goyim* (translated in the Septuagint as *ethne* and by Jerome as *gentes*) are biological. Much of the books of Genesis and Exodus are concerned with these biological roots of ancestry. The genealogies and the story of Babel present explanations for diversity in spite of the original unity of the human race. While similar in most respects to the Greco-Roman sense of *ethnos,* they differ in that they present the descent of whole "peoples," rather than just the leading families from particular individuals, thus making the various peoples of Scripture even more homogeneous than those of Greco-Roman ethnography. As in the case of the barbarian *gentes,* membership in the *goyim* is presumably objective and immutable. The *goyim* of Scripture and the *ethne* or *gentes* of classical ethnographers are virtually identical. They belong to the eternal natural world, not the world of history.

The other model is that of the *am* (translated as *laos, populus*), the people of Israel, a constitutional body like that of Rome. Just as Romulus took the *multitudo* of Albans and Latins and through law formed them into a people, through the covenant on Mount Sinai, the descendants of Israel become the people of Israel or of God. Nor will all the descendants of Israel be heirs of the covenant. Both are constitutionally rather than biologically determined groups.

The constitutional nature of the people of Israel is not always reflected in the heterogeneous books that make up the Hebrew scriptures. In the books of *Esdras* and *Nehemiah,* the children of Israelites who had married alien wives were excluded from those who returned from captivity. Here one sees the origins of an exclusive, biological definition of the chosen people. Still, at least for the later prophets, membership in the *am* is not limited to the biological descendants of Abraham, Isaac, and Jacob. The sons of Abraham can be all people who accept the covenant, just as the *populus Romanus* can be open to all.

Social Identity in Christian Antiquity

Christian authors of Late Antiquity inherited both the biblical and classical traditions of ethnography. They synthesized them to form a new understanding of human society. The Christian Scriptures emphasized still further the unimportance of inherited ethnic, social, and legal status. The new people of God was not bound by any traditional ethnic or, indeed, legal or gender category. The final commission of Christ was to "Go forth and teach all nations (*ethne*)" (Matt. 28, 18). Paul wrote, "There is neither Jew nor Greek, there is neither slave nor free, there is neither male nor female, for you are all one in Christ Jesus"(Gal. 3, 28). The people of God thus unites all without distinction.

Of course, not all received the message of the Gospel, and by the fourth century Christian thinkers, themselves thoroughly Roman in their education and patterns of thought, had to deal with a world that retained the distinctions of inclusion and exclusion long familiar to Jews and Romans alike. Jerome, implicitly in his translation of the Bible, and Augustine, explicitly in his *City of God,* blended the Roman and Jewish ethnographies into one.

The *ethne* or *goyim* are still present in both, with their biological origins, their objective status, and their ahistorical continuity. In contrast, the people of God, the Israelites of the Old Testament and the Christians of the New, possess the characteristics of a people in the Roman and Jewish traditions. While the distinction is not always as clear in the use of terminology as some have suggested, the Latin fathers saw the citizens of the City of God in terms of a constitutionally structured community, which, like those of Rome and Israel, was based on law and contract.[19]

For Augustine, the third age of the world, the time from Abraham to David, is the period of the ethnogenesis of the Israelites. It is the time of election, of separation of the people of God from the *gentes,* of the pact with Abraham, of the exile, and of the exodus.[20] Through these experiences—and, in particular, through the renewal of the covenant on Sinai, the years of wandering, the political organization into tribes, and the conquest of Canaan—the people of Israel was born.

While the people of God is the one perfect *populus,* since it alone is founded on true justice and proper love, Augustine is willing to recognize that secular societies, too, share characteristics of peoplehood. However, while the Roman tradition dichotomized Romans and others, the Christian interpretation placed them, at least in theory, on the same plane. The Roman *populus* as well as those of "the Athenians, those of any other Greeks, of the Egyptians, of that earlier Babylon of the Assyrians and of any other *gens* whatsoever" were genuine *populi* since each was "united in fellowship by common agreement about the objects of its love."[21]

Thus by the beginning of the fifth century, inhabitants of the Roman world, whether Christian, Jewish, or pagan, knew two models of peoplehood—one that we shall call *ethnic,* based on descent, custom, and territory; one *constitutional,* based on law and adhesion. No consistent vocabulary separated the two, and no clear set of characteristics distinguished between them. The difference was largely one of perspective. The internal observer— whether Roman, Jew, or Christian—saw the complexities and heterogeneous nature of his community. Membership in it was determined both by the community's acceptance of the individual and the individual's willingness to accept the community's laws and values. Thus, membership was, at least in part, subjective and contingent.

In contrast to this "we" group, the same individual, viewing others, saw homogeneity, simplicity, and ahistoricity. At best, Rome, the Greek cities of the Classical Age, and perhaps the great Empires of Persia and Egypt could be seen as constitutional bodies based on law and common purpose. But the other model—that of mythical descent, of biological and immutable categorization based on geography, language, and custom—prevailed, particularly when looking outside of *Romanitas* at the barbarian *gentes* that surrounded and increasingly threatened it. This distinction was not made according to recognized realities of social or cultural organization but the inherited prejudices of centuries since the rejection of Herodotus's nonjudgmental inquiry into the peoples of the known world.

Classical Ethnography and the Barbarian Migrations

The historians of Late Antiquity, particularly Ammianus Marcellinus, Procopius, and Priscus, sensed the contradictions between the received tradition and their own personal experiences with the barbarian peoples who transformed the Empire between the third and sixth centuries. Unlike an armchair ethnographer, such as Pliny, whose ignorance and distance allowed him to classify the peoples of the world in a comprehensive and authoritative system almost unencumbered by contact with reality, their contacts with these *gentes* was prolonged and intimate. The messiness of reality inevitably collided with the neatness of theory.

When, for example, Ammianus depicts the Roman emperor Julian's campaigns against the Alamanni in the fourth century, he is aware that the Alamanni form a complex confederation. They are led by seven kings, of whom the two principals, Chnodomarius and Serapio, he says, exercise a power beyond that of the others. But this army is not a single *gens Alamannorum*. Rather, it is assembled "from various nations (*nationibus*), in part by greed, in part by mutual assistance treaty."[22] Procopius begins his description of the Goths by explaining that "There were many Gothic nations in the past as there are now," and then lists the most important of these *ethne* as the Goths, the Vandals, the Visigoths, and the Gepaedes.[23] When Priscus visited the court of Attila, he described the Huns as a composite, made up of various peoples speaking Hunnic, Gothic, and Latin.[24]

And yet so powerful was the weight of tradition that even these firsthand observers could not free themselves from the assumptions of classical ethnography. Ammianus, for example, had personal knowledge of the Alamanni and other frontier peoples in the West, yet he frequently referred to them simply as the *Germani* or the *barbari;* he did not count Eastern peoples such as the Goths among the *Germani*—the term had a geographical, not a linguistic meaning. Procopius, after distinguishing the variety of Goths, returned to tradition to announce that their ancient names were Sauromatae and Melanchlaeni, two peoples from Herodotus, and then went on to say that they were also known as the Getic *ethne.* Actually, he said, they differed only in their names; in appearance, laws, and religion, they were exactly the same.[25] Clearly, in spite of the detail of his information, he was still a prisoner of the classical ethnographic literature that came before him.

Why did he fail to allow experience to take precedence over tradition and to recognize in other peoples the same complexities in his own? Arrogance and cultural chauvinism were important, of course. Ignorance played a part, no doubt, as did deep prejudice toward all that was non-Roman. But his view was also in part a practical one: Roman imperialists found it easier to deal with others as though they were homogeneous ethnic peoples than to acknowledge that the "other" could be as complex and fluid as Romans themselves. Communities that absolutely defied such neat categorizations—especially Jews and Christians who shared the traditional Roman dichotomous view of the world but placed themselves rather than the Romans at the center—were especially frustrating. The Emperor Marcus Aurelius, commenting on his dealings with the Jews, supposedly said, "O you Marcomanni, you Quadi, you Sarmatians. At last I have found another even more disorderly than you." Echoing him, Julian, complaining to the Christians, would say, "Listen to me, whom the Alamanni and Franks heard."[26] The implication was that if only Jews and Christians could behave like barbarian *gentes,* all would be well in the Empire. The problem was, of course, that the barbarian *gentes* themselves did not conform to the patterns imputed to them by the Romans either.

Despite Roman categorizations, the barbarian peoples whose entry into the Roman world transformed it so profoundly were, like the Romans, constitutional rather than ethnic polities, uniting groups of diverse cultural, linguistic, and geographical origins under the leadership of aristocratic warrior families. The Alamanni, the Goths, the Alans, the Huns, the Franks, and others were composed of groups speaking a variety of languages, following various customs, and identifying themselves with varying traditions.

They also seem to have appeared and disappeared with considerable rapidity, although their tendency to assume the names of earlier "peoples," and the tendency of Romans to identify new "peoples" with names culled from Herodotus, Pliny, or other ancient authorities made them appear more lasting than they actually were. Finally, as they came into the Roman orbit, their political, social, and economic structures were molded by Roman civilization even as their self-perceptions were deeply influenced by the systems of classification of their Roman neighbors, whose customs they sought to assimilate.

The Peoples of Europe in Late Antiquity

Depending on the system of social classification one selects, one can categorize the inhabitants of Europe in the first centuries of the Empire in various overlapping and, even, contradictory manners.

A traditional distinction within the free population of the Empire through the second century had been that of citizen and noncitizen. In the first century, this had been a vital separating line, which did not necessarily follow either language, *ethnos,* or geography, as the story of St. Paul's claim to citizenship and its consequences illustrates. The limits of citizenship and hence of Roman law did, however, in general, depend on province and *civitas,* so that restricted citizenship reinforced pre-Roman regional, political, and cultural distinctions. However, after 212, when citizenship was extended to virtually all free inhabitants of the Empire—pagans and Jews alike—largely as a revenue-producing measure, this distinction meant nothing. What mattered was a social distinction, based largely on wealth and political clout, between *honestiores,* those members of the elite who had automatic access to the emperor against capital charges, and the *humiliores,* the mass of citizens who were subject to the authority of provincial governors without hope of appeal.

The universalization of citizenship also led to the substantial abolition of non-Roman legal traditions in favor of universal Roman law. While this extension never entirely eliminated regional variations in law, particularly in the Hellenized East, it weakened the significance of provincial identities. Although, throughout the history of the Empire and beyond, elite individuals continued to identify closely with their *civitas,* this kind of local, emotional attachment was supplemental to, rather than in place of, a self-identity as a Roman. Nor was this identity a defensive one, pitting one community against another. Rather, it manifested itself in a kind of local pride, expressed in the praise of the fertile countryside, its natural advantages, crops, and traditions.

As central government faded, these local identities, expressed in terms at once derived from Roman civil subdivisions and from pre-Roman "ethnic" vocabulary, came to dominate the rhetoric of provincial discourse. In Gaul, where Roman administrative units followed to some extent the outlines of local tribal areas, these tribal names re-emerged as the favored designations for local identity.

Likewise, as imperial governance faded from the West, the Romano-barbarian elites sought to place the new political and social realities into the perspective of inherited political and ethnographic tradition. Far from rejecting the facile images of ethnicity, elaborated through centuries of classical writing, they internalized them, accepting the characteristics that Romans had long projected onto barbarians as reality. The result was that both within the barbarian kingdoms and in Constantinople, these new polities, with their barbarian rulers, were understood as the "other" in the terminology inherited from Greco-Roman ethnography. Throughout the former Empire, the ruling elites both perceived themselves and were perceived as *gentes,* united under an ethnic king by common descent, language, and custom. Still, these new elites sought parity between their *gens* and the *populus Romanus.* The result was a transformation of how both social categories were understood.

Equality demanded equal antiquity, learning, and virtue. The "new" peoples that had appeared on the frontiers of the Empire thus had to be given a history as ancient and glorious as that of the Romans. The Trojan origins of Rome had provided such a background for Roman history vis-à-vis Greek history. Jewish and later Christian apologists had faced the same problem and had resolved it by establishing the history of the Hebrew people within a context of Greco-Roman history, positing not only equality but long contact and borrowing by Greek philosophers and lawgivers from the Hebrew patriarchs and prophets. In the first known attempt to re-evaluate a barbarian people, Cassidorius apparently took the same approach, culling ancient authors for descriptions of peoples who might have been Goths and weaving Gothic oral traditions into universal, that is, Greco-Roman history, on behalf of his Ostrogothic rulers. He claimed that, in his now-lost Gothic history, he had "made the Gothic origin Roman history."[27] What exactly this meant has long been the subject of much debate. It certainly meant much more than one historian's attempt to explain that

Cassidorius had simply recounted Gothic history as "serial biography" in the manner of Roman historians.[28] By establishing seventeen generations of Gothic kings (the same number that separated Aeneas and Romulus), by discovering their deeds in (Greek and Latin) books rather than merely in oral tradition, he showed that the Goths, although barbarians, belonged to the same world as the Romans. In the early sections of Jordanes's *Getica*—drawn, in part at least, from Cassidorus's lost work—the Goths, identified with the Getae of classical historiography, knew valorous warriors and virtuous kings of the family of the Amals, and cultivated philosophy and theology even before they entered the Roman orbit.

Jordanes's version of the incorporation of the Goths into classical historiography provided the model followed by all subsequent historians of "barbarian histories." Whatever other political, religious, or literary agendas they may have been following, authors of what are loosely termed *Origines gentium* from the sixth to the twelfth centuries routinely brought their peoples onto the stage of Greco-Roman history as early as possible, drawing for this purpose on ancient ethnography and Roman history, when they did not make their peoples themselves descend directly from Trojan heroes.

But at the same time that the elites of the barbarian kingdoms were internalizing Roman traditions about barbarians, they were erasing the long-treasured distinction between Roman and barbarian. This is the explicit intent of Jordanes, who completes his *Getica* with the unification of the Amal and Ancii brought about with the birth of Germanus Posthumus, son of the last Amal and nephew of the Emperor Justinian. The reduction of Romans and Goths to two families, which could be merged by a fortuitous marriage alliance, carried implications not only for the understanding of barbarian *ethne* but for that of the Romans as well. By the sixth century, the *populus Romanus* was seen, at least by people such as Jordanes, as qualitatively the same as a barbarian *gens*. The dis-

61

tinctions between "them" and "us" were disappearing. Certainly, the idea of a Roman *gens* was not foreign to Roman thought: Poets such as Virgil could speak of the great effort that had gone into founding the Roman *gens*. And yet, the old sense that such social groups could indeed be founded and thus were outside the natural order of birth and descent (as in the more organic notion of *natio*) was fading. Romans were becoming a *gens* like their barbarian neighbors and successors.

At the same time that Romans were becoming more of a *gens,* the barbarians were becoming more of a *populus.* The transformation of ethnic labeling from a "them" to an "us" category in the context of the barbarian kingdoms thus placed a new emphasis on the political nature of peoples, something that had been a minor element in classical ethnography but the decisive element in Roman constitutional identity. Membership in a barbarian people depended more on willingness to identify with the traditions of that people—incarnated in its political leadership, that is, royal or aristocratic families, and its ability to contribute to that tradition, essentially through military service—than on biological descent, culture, language, or geographical origin. It is to this complex, contradictory, and fascinating process of creating European peoples, both in the minds of intellectuals and on the land of the Roman Empire, that we now turn.

Chapter Three

Barbarians and Other Romans

Romans loved to juxtapose themselves and their world against that of the barbarians. But as we suggested in the previous chapter, the two categories were hardly commensurate: Roman identity in the sense of *populus Romanus* was a constitutional one, internally generated and based on a common cultural and intellectual tradition, a legal system, and a willingness to be part of a common economic and political tradition. In brief, *Roman* was a constitutional, not an ethnic category in any meaningful sense of the term. *Barbarian,* by contrast, was an invented category, projected onto a variety of peoples with all the prejudices and assumptions of centuries of classical ethnography and imperialism. Nor, in spite of the emphasis placed by Romans on the gulf separating the two, were they necessarily mutually exclusive. One might be both a Roman and a barbarian. The distinction, always more theoretical than real, became ever more blurred in the fourth and fifth centuries.

Class, Regional, and Religious Identity in the Empire

Nor was *Roman* a primary self-identifier for the millions of people who inhabited, permanently or temporarily, the Roman Empire. Rather than sharing a national or ethnic identity, individuals were more likely to feel a primary attachment to class, occupation, or city. Certainly from the early third century, citizenship counted for little. Since 212 C.E., virtually all the inhabitants of the Empire were Roman citizens, a once-coveted status (remember Paul's pride when he could announce, to a Roman officer who had acquired his citizenship at great price, that he, Paul, was a Roman from birth), it had now become a simple fiscal and military expediency. The Emperor Caracalla had extended Roman citizenship to all so that all would be eligible for service in the legions and so that all would have to pay inheritance taxes owed only by citizens.

With virtually every free person living in the Empire a Roman, self-identification as "Roman" lost its importance. Modern ethnographic studies of identity have demonstrated that it is most often those at the borders of groups who generate important "ethnic" identities, largely in opposition to the "other" with whom they, unlike those at the center, constantly interact. But, since the majority of Roman citizens lived surrounded by other citizens, since most never looked across the Danube at "Free Germans" or risked the sands of the Sahara to encounter Berber tribesmen, their Romanness was less important than other factors in determining their core identity. The real solidarities (and oppositions) derived from class, regional, occupational, and, in some limited circumstances, religious differences. Barbarians existed, when they existed at all, as a theoretical category but not as a part of lived experience.

The great divide in the Roman world lay between those who were slaves and those who were free. The Empire had always been a slave-based society and one in which slaves—whether drawn from outside the Empire through foreign wars or from within by inherited status or punishment—provided most of the agricultural, craft, and industrial labor. Slaves were subject to the whims of their masters and were protected only by their economic value. And, yet, no clear-cut racial, ethnic, or religious boundary separated master from slave. True, some slaves were recent imports from sub-Saharan Africa or the forests of Germany, and both were prized and distinguished by their skin color, size, and exotic appearance. Most, however, were indistinguishable from the mass of the population except, perhaps, by brands or tattoos marking their slave status, or else scars from beatings by their masters.

The divide between a slave and a free person was, in theory, absolute, but it was also permeable. Just as free men and women could sink into slavery through criminal or civil justice, slaves found and did carve out a sphere in the domains of free society and could, in time, rise out of their slavery. Roman slaves might be allowed by their masters to have their own property, termed their *peculium,* that they earned in their free time. Although normally a token amount, this could, in rare cases, make it possible for slaves to buy their freedom and that of their families. Failing this, Romans had long practiced public displays of generosity by enfranchising slaves, often at their deaths, so that their funeral rites might be observed by crowds of grateful mourners.

Freed slaves lived in an intermediate world, free before the law and able to act independently toward the rest of society, but still bound by specific obligations of deference, payments, and support to their former masters. In theory, at least, the status of freedman was not inherited by children: The grandsons of slaves could rise as high as their luck and talents might take them. Spectacular ascents seldom happened, but enough did to maintain the dream of upward mobility from slavery to riches and the possibility, however rarely taken, of moving from the status of object to that of person before the law.

65

Among the free citizens of the Empire, the gulfs separating the elite and the masses of the population were enormous. Ordinary peasants, working the land of others as sharecroppers or tenant farmers, might be barely indistinguishable from slaves. The elites, or *honestiores,* enjoyed legally protected rights by virtue of their wealth and value to the Roman state. Unlike the *humiliores,* or ordinary citizens, they were exempt from corporal punishment, the most burdensome and humiliating obligation of the masses. As for the ordinary citizens, from a purely economic position, they might be worse off than privileged slaves and had nothing in common with the rich landowners who controlled most aspects of their lives. During the third century, under the pressure of taxation, military recruitment, and population decline, the status of tenant farmers or *colons* increasingly came to resemble that of slaves. Since landlords were required to collect taxes from their estates and empty land did not yield any taxes, landlords were given the authority to control their labor force. Agricultural work (like other professions) became hereditary. Landlords were authorized to pursue fugitive tenants and to force them to return to their estates. Increasingly, in the third and fourth centuries, landlords exercised a kind of authority over their tenants that included not only traditional Roman patronage rights, but greater political power as well.

The landowners of the Empire monopolized economic power and political prestige at a local and regional level. In every corner of the Empire, members of municipal councils, their positions secured by landed wealth, dominated public life. It was they who profited most directly from the Roman system of government and the "free trade zone" that made up the Roman world. At the same time, they had obligations, the most important of them being the collection, through agents, of the annual tax assessment. A portion of this tax went to the imperial treasury; the remainder stayed in the community for public services. Local council members determined who paid what portions of these assessments and how these local funds would be used, and thereby built and increased their own patronage networks. As long as these taxes could be collected at no great cost to themselves, such service was a prime goal of aspiring local gentry.

These elites were not simply distinguished from the masses by their wealth. With wealth came culture, *paideia*, which more than any other characteristic marked what it meant to be not merely Roman but civilized. Through education, cultivated as part of the lifestyle of the provincial elite, *honestiores* developed their identity as part of the wider world of Roman culture.

But however wide the cultural worlds that *paideia* opened to them, most local elites remained fiercely attached to the regions in which they owned their estates. From Syria to Gaul, North Africa to the Danubian frontier, local landowners remained deeply rooted to the particularities of their region or *patria*. The reasons for this are numerous. The Empire had been, since its inception, a network of cities (and their surrounding territories), bound by specific treaties to the city of Rome. Many local notables were descendants of regional elites whose families had dominated local society from before the arrival of the Roman Empire. As much as possible, Roman imperial expansion had always drawn pre-existing local powers into the Roman orbit. In the pluralistic religious and cultural tradition of Rome, the central state had never demanded exclusive adherence to Roman values: Whenever possible, local tradition was assimilated into or equated with that of Rome. However, one did not need to forget one's pre-Roman family position in earlier tribal or cultural traditions. These could and did become points of pride for provincial notables. Thus, becoming Roman didn't mean abandoning old ways for new; rather, it meant discovering the old in the new.

The same process of social and political absorption operated in the religious sphere. From Mesopotamia to Britain, new gods could be worshiped as local manifestations of the old and the familiar. The Celtic deity Teutates became subsumed into Mercury; Hercules often appeared in Asia Minor as a Phoenician or Punic god. Perhaps the most outstanding example of such syncretism was Isis who, in Apuleius's *Metamorphoses* explains that the Phrygians call her Pessinuntia, the mother God; the Athenians Pallas Athena; the Cyprians Venus Paphia; the Cretans Diana; the Sicilians Prosperpina; the Elusinians Ceres; while others call her Juno, Bello, Hecata, Nemefin, and so on.[1] Different peoples were united in their worship, even if they were unaware of it.

The only serious exception to Rome's ability to absorb religions into its own was Judaism and, to a lesser extent, its offshoot, Christianity. Radical monotheism posed an insurmountable problem to Roman religious policy. Some Jews could and did become Romans, as the example of Paul shows. However, they could not be fully bound into the Roman world by the traditional ties of religion. Still, after the final destruction of the temple in 70 C.E. and the expulsion from Palestine and Judea, those Jews who remained scattered across the Empire seem to have made their peace with the imperial system. There were no longer reports of separatist or seditious behavior on the part of these small, dispersed communities. Instead, such subversive behavior was practiced by the Christians.

They, too, were radical monotheists, whose rejection of the traditional cults of Rome as well as the Romanized cults of the Empire earned them a reputation as dangerous atheists. However, unlike the Jews, Christians identified themselves with no single geographical region or social class. Christian communities were notorious for ignoring the normal standards of social status. Each community developed as a local *ecclesia* or assembly, centered, like the rest of the Roman world, on its city and directed by its locally elected bishop. The "churches" of Antioch, Alexandria, or Rome were hardly uniform. And yet Christians were, at the same time, part of a sect that transcended the particularisms of the late Empire, one of the few movements that embraced a universal culture that paradoxically transcended the local traditions of every local church. Christians thus presented the anomaly of a brotherhood at once local and universal, its members ordinary citizens and at the same time profoundly alienated from their neighbors. This very lack of clearly distinguishing characteristics by which members of this sect could be identified outside the religious sphere may have contributed to the irrational fears they evoked in ordinary people as well as in the defenders of the imperial order.

Christians insisted that they were entirely like their fellow citizens: dutiful, moral, and loyal supporters of the emperor, of their cities, of their classes and occupations. And yet their beliefs radically separated them from the sacred bonds that integrated the Roman world.

Religious integration was only part of the process by which local magnates had been absorbed into the Roman world without uprooting them from their former alliances. Marriage and kinship ties bound Roman elites to their cities and provinces as well. Roman veterans and bureaucrats retired to newly founded colonies where they intermarried with local families, bringing with them Roman cultural traditions but being themselves absorbed into the agrarian economies of provincial towns. Local men who achieved great success in the wider world of the Empire often retired to their hometowns to take on the honors and the duties of local patrons. Newcomers and old families blended together, sustaining the local landowning elite. Over generations, the networks of intermarriage among local families deepened the identity with the local landscape and tradition. Such local identities did not replace or even compete with *Romanitas*. Indeed, *Romanitas* was the necessary context within which the particularities of provincial identity could flourish.

Roman aristocratic identity thus was multilayered. Through the rigorous tradition of aristocratic education, Roman elites came to identify fully with the central Roman traditions, to recognize in Virgil, in Cicero, in Horace, their own pasts. At the same time, they remained firmly attached to their province and especially to their city. They praised its beauty, its fertility, and its rivers and forests in their poetry. They sought their future in its markets and in public roles in its local senate or curia. They worshiped in its temples, which were at once as universal as Rome and as local as the landscape that they loved.

Some historians, concentrating on the brutal gulfs separating slave and free person, tenant farmer and landowner, assume that class identity was far more important to these groups than regional, ethnic, or social solidarities. In a certain sense this is surely true: The economic and legal realities of life in the late Empire militated against strong vertical bonds in society, and sporadic violence, usually in opposition to oppressive landlords, was common. However, the gulf separating social strata was never so great that it could not be breached, through social mobility or through patronage networks.

Throughout its history, the Roman Empire offered the possibility, however theoretical, of social mobility, from slave to senator. No matter how lowly one's lot, advancement was always a theoretical, if not a real, possibility. In the protracted crisis of the third century, such moves, generally through military service, were more than just a distant possibility: The Emperor Diocletian was himself the son of a Dalmatian freedman. Diocletian's chosen successor, Galerius (305–311), came from similarly modest origins: He began life as a cattle herder in the Carpathian mountains.

Even if most peasants did not rise from obscurity to great power, they remained connected to their betters through bonds of patronage and clientship, one of the most ancient bonds in Roman society. In the provinces, where conquered societies lived, similar bonds overlay the relationship between landlords and their peasants and dependents. In the troubled times of Late Antiquity, the importance of these bonds for both sides of the spectrum increased, as peasants looked to their patrons for protection from imperial tax collectors and army recruiters, and landlords sought to raise their own militias from among the inhabitants of their estates. In the fifth century, revolts against the imperial government were mounted not only by slaves and *coloni* but by their patrons as well. However, no evidence suggests that such solidarities amounted to anything bordering on ethnic or national identification: They were loyalties to individuals or families.

The Roman Center

Of course, members of some families were more than local magnates and regional power brokers. The great families of the Empire held lands in many provinces: vast estates in Africa, in Gaul, and, if they were to be in the Roman Senate, necessarily in Italy itself. These families, operating at the highest level of imperial life, were bearers of a fullness of Roman tradition, which might mean the rejection or suppression of their provincial roots. Through the second century, these families tended to be Italian, if not in origins, then in residence and in self-identification. Although their income might come from the far corners of the Empire, it moved, as in ages past, toward the city of Rome.

The only access to such status, or the surest way to maintain it through generations, was through imperial service. Until late in the third century, the career path of public service for young aristocrats who hoped to rise through to the highest ranks of power and wealth, lay in alternating civil and military duties. Service in the imperial system, like service in a modern multinational corporation, meant constant movement. A young man zigzagged across the Empire as he rose through military and civil office toward ever-higher honors. Italy and the city of Rome continued to draw the ambitious and the wealthy. The cradle of Roman civiliza-

71

tion continued to be the epicenter for the creation and distribution of the apparently inexhaustible resources offered those who were willing and able to be fully Roman.

Nevertheless, such local boys who made good were not forgotten by their hometowns. The hundreds of inscriptions on the bases of statues erected to such figures across the Empire by the towns of their birth and/or by the communities in which they retired testify to the continuing local ties binding even those who rose to dizzying heights. Even a god-emperor like Diocletian could eventually retire, in imperial splendor of course, to his native Illyricum.

If the great senatorial families comprised one center of Romanness, the military provided the other. In some respects, the military represented a different kind of identity, one less tied to the particularities of a region. Roman legions were drawn from throughout the Empire and stationed in strategic border regions. Although auxiliaries had been recruited from among neighboring peoples since the first century, normal practice was to divide these units up and to distribute them throughout the Empire, preferably as far from their kin and people as possible. Thus, Germanic troops found their way to Egypt while Scyths were garrisoned in Gaul and Britain. Both for populations living on the fringe of the Empire and for the auxiliary troops from beyond these fringes stationed far from home and kin, the army was the primary vehicle of Romanization, the only truly Roman institution in the Empire.

This separate identity began to change in the Empire in the third century. The extension of citizenship opened the legions to virtually the entire population, and legions recruited locally in the districts where they were stationed, often for decades or even centuries. Moreover, already from the late second century, active duty soldiers were allowed to marry (although they had already been doing this informally for decades). Their wives, drawn from the local population, accelerated the process by which the military merged into the local community to such an extent that attempts to move legions across the Empire to meet the threat of invasion could result in revolt. Auxiliaries, too, resisted any attempt to transfer them from their homes. In 360, faced with a massive Persian attack on the Eastern front, Emperor Constantius ordered auxiliaries and other troops from the Germanic frontier east: The result was open revolt by troops who proclaimed the Western Caesar Julian emperor.

Social Identities in the Barbarian World

Across the frontiers of this vast Empire, the Roman troops kept vigil on the world they were eager to term *barbarian.*

Romans called the social units of their barbarian neighbors *gentes* (Greek, *ethne*), "peoples," and ascribed to them all the immutable characteristics that had been, as we have seen, part of classical ethnography since Herodotus. What exactly these groups were, what their own self-identity or "ethnic consciousness," if any, may have been, is impossible to ascertain. By observing them, through the eyes of their Roman neighbors, however, we can reach some conclusions that are at odds with the image of their "civilized" contemporaries.

Barbarians consisted of small communities of farmers and herders living in villages along rivers, seacoasts, and clearings from the North and Baltic Seas to the Black Sea. Most members of these societies were free men and women, organized in nuclear households governed by the husband or father. Status within the village depended on wealth, measured by the size of a family's cattle herd, and military prowess. Some wealthier men presided over households that included not only their wife or wives and children, but free dependents and slaves housed in outbuildings around the leader's home.

Households were, in turn, integrated into the larger kindred known to scholars as the sip or clan. This wider circle of kin in-

73

cluded both paternal and maternal kin groups, who shared a perception of common descent reinforced by a special "peace" that made violent conflict within the clan a crime for which no compensation or atonement could be made. Clans also had an incest taboo and possibly some claims to inheritance. This wider kindred might also form the basis for mutual defense and for pursuing feuds. However, membership in this larger circle was elastic. It provided the possibility but not the necessity of concerted action, since individuals might select from a variety of possible broader kin affiliations, depending on circumstances. The nuclear family, not the wider clan, was the primary unit of barbarian society.

Village life was directed by the assembly of free men under the leadership of a headman whose position may have come from a combination of factors, including his wealth, family influence, and connections with the supra-village leadership, that is, the people. Beyond the village level, wider constellations, *gentes*, or peoples, were bound together by a combination of religious, legal, and political traditions that imparted a strong, if unstable, sense of unity.

Members of a "people" shared common ancestry myths, cultural traditions, a legal system, and leaders. However, all of these were flexible, multiple, and subject to negotiation and even dispute. Ancestry myths took the form of genealogies of heroic figures and their exploits. The founders of these genealogies were divine, and the chain of their descendants did not form a history in the Greco-Roman sense of a structured narrative of events and their broader significance. Rather, these myths preserved an atemporal and apolitical account of individuals, woven together through ties of kinship and tales of revenge and blood feud, to which many individuals and families could claim ties.

Scholars have termed these complexes of traditional beliefs "kernels of tradition" and, since the work of the German medieval historian and ethnologist Reinhard Wenskus, have argued that royal families were the bearers of this *traditionskern* and embodied in it the essence of a fictive but dynamic ethnic identity.[2] In many cases, this was so. However, it is equally possible that differing families maintained differing or competing versions of traditions and sought to impose their versions and, hence, their authority over their communities at the expense of others. In still other cases, such traditions were probably much more widely diffused within society rather than being the exclusive property of individual families. Certainly, when individuals in the course of the fourth and fifth centuries managed to establish themselves in positions of dominance, they laid claim to these traditions or associated themselves with glorious legendary families and heroes of myth. In so doing, they attempted to make their history that of the people. At times this proved successful; at other times disastrous.

Other cultural traditions, too, such as language, arms, tactics, dress, and hairstyles, could provide bonds uniting social groups, but these were also fluid and adaptable ways of creating unity or claiming difference.[3] Even Romans recognized that while an ideal schema separated people by language, there were more peoples than there were languages. Nor did anyone prior to the ninth century seem to recognize the linguistic unity of the Germanic languages spoken by many of the barbarian peoples.

Weapons and tactics varied among barbarians, although the extent to which these were important to specific barbarian peoples as signs of unity is similarly uncertain. Distinctive weapons or tactics such as Hunnic bows, Dacian javelins, Gothic lances, or Frankish axes appear in Roman sources, but without any real consistency. These references may have been more a reflection of the Roman mania for classification than of actual barbarian practice. Even in the case of the Frankish ax, which seems, indeed, to have been a characteristic weapon by the end of the fifth century, the Franks themselves seem to have been less aware of it as a "Frankish" tradition than were their enemies, the Visigoths and the Byzantines.

Similarly, distinctions between Scythic peoples (Goths, Huns, and Avars), who fought on horseback, and Germans and Celts, who fought on foot, were exaggerated by Roman sources: Certainly steppe nomads were mounted warriors, but so too were western Germanic warriors when their wealth and status allowed it. Moreover, as barbarian units were recruited into the Roman army, they may have been given specialized roles that corresponded more to Roman military needs than to traditional ethnic strengths. The *notitia dignitatum,* an official list of high military and civil officers from around 400, lists cavalry units composed of Alamanni and Franks. Were these warriors recruited into the imperial army because of their cavalry skills, or did they specialize in mounted warfare in response to Roman needs?

Clothing and ornamentation certainly varied widely and may have been symbols of group identity. How certain members of a society dressed, what sorts of brooches or belts they wore, how they styled their hair could all have important symbolic meaning. What such meanings were is impossible to discern in retrospect. Romans delighted in commenting on distinctions of dress and hairstyle, but, again, this may correspond more to Roman interests in classification than in accuracy of observation. It is perhaps best to conclude that these characteristics could be manipulated and adjusted to meet the changing interests of group formation, rather than viewing them as evidence of immutable cultural solidarity.

Legal traditions—that is, ways of dealing with conflicts—were an outgrowth of religious and cultural identity. With very weak central authority, disputes were regulated through family leaders, village assemblies, and military leaders. Controls were designed to preserve peace or at least set the rules according to which the feud could take place in a manner least destructive to the community. Finally, these religious and cultural groups were organized under political leadership, a leadership that, in the early centuries of contact with Rome, underwent profound transformation.

When the Romans first came into contact with the Celtic and Germanic peoples, these populations were largely governed by hereditary, sacral kings, who embodied the identity of their people. In the course of the first and second centuries, those living in proximity to the Romans had largely abandoned their traditional sacral kings in favor of warrior leaders who might be selected from old royal families or, just as frequently, from the ranks of successful fighters. This change favored the Empire, since Rome could more easily influence new leaders emerging from oligarchic factions than heirs of ancient religious authority.

These leaders were elevated by their heterogeneous armies and formed the centers around which new traditions of political and religious identity could develop, and onto which, in some cases, older notions of sacrosocial identity could be grafted. The legitimacy of these leaders derived ultimately from their ability to lead their armies to victory. A victorious campaign confirmed their right to rule and drew to them an ever-growing people who accepted and shared in their identity. With luck, it also brought Roman recognition and support. Thus, a charismatic leader could be the beginning of a new people. In time, the leader and his descendants might identify themselves with an older tradition and claim divine sanction, proven by their fortunes in war, to embody and perpetuate some ancient "people." The constitutional integrity of these peoples, then, was dependent on warfare and conquest for their identity and continuity: They were armies, although their economies remained dependent on raiding and a combination of animal husbandry and slash-and-burn agriculture. Defeat, at the hands of either the Romans or other barbarians, could mean not only the end of a ruler but the end of a people, which might then be absorbed into another, more victorious confederation.

But, by the third century, the Empire had even transformed the populations of Europe living outside its frontiers. Roman policy dictated the creation of client buffer-states that could protect the

Empire from contact with hostile barbarians farther afield; provide trading partners for the supply of cattle, raw materials, and
slaves; and auxiliary troops. This was nothing new. For centuries,
the Empire had supported friendly chieftains, supplying them with
weapons, gold, and grain in order to strengthen the pro-Roman
factions within the barbarian world. Some were rewarded with citizenship. Arminius, the famous victor over Varus in the Teuto-
burger Forest, was himself not only a citizen but had even been ad-
mitted to the ranks of the equestrian order.[4]

The effect of Roman proximity, not only on the barbarians living along the *limes* but on those farther away, was considerable.
Roman economic and political power destabilized the rough balance of power within the barbarian world by enabling pro-Roman
chieftains to accumulate wealth and power far in excess of what
had been possible previously. These chieftains, endowed with citizenship and taught the ways of Roman taxation, also gained both
military and political experience by serving in the Roman military
system with their troops as federates. At the same time, fear of the
Romans and their allies drove anti-Roman factions into large, unstable, but, occasionally, mighty confederations that could inflict
considerable damage on Roman interests on both sides of the borders. This had happened in the time of Caesar among the Gauls
and at the end of the first century among the Britons. In the late
second century, a broad confederacy known as the Marcomanni
tested and temporarily broke the Danubian frontier.

At any given time, therefore, within these broad confederations,
a variety of individuals might claim some sort of kingship over portions of the "people," proposing that their own traditions should
form the "kernel of tradition" around which a group should ad-
here, or else claiming that they were the legitimate bearers of an
ancient, shared tradition. Seen in this light, "ethnic" identity among
barbarians was extraordinarily fluid, as new groups emerged and
old ones disappeared. What remained, often, was the belief, how-

ever imaginary, that the group possessed an ancient and divinely sanctioned past.

Crisis and Restoration

In the course of the third century, pressures both internal and external introduced a fundamental restructuring of the society and institutions both within and outside the Empire. The results were far-reaching and changed not only the social structures of the people of Late Antiquity but also their self-perceptions. Old solidarities dissolved and new identities, some harkening back to ancient, pre-Roman identities, emerged.

The Crisis of the Third Century was a complex phenomenon, brought on by increased pressures on the frontiers of the Danube, North Africa, and Sassanid Persia as well as by population decrease and a crisis of leadership within the traditional, Italian-based center of Roman power. Whatever its ultimate causes, it resulted in a shift in the balance of power from Italy to the frontiers, where the army faced the challenge of retaining the barbarians. Emperors were no longer created in the old centers of the Empire but rather raised up by frontier troops from among their commanders. When these "barracks emperors" proved unable to meet the soldiers' demands for higher pay or to lead them to victory against rival armies or barbarian foes, they were assassinated by their own troops. Between 235 and 284, seventeen of the twenty emperors met violent deaths, often after only a few months of disputed rule.

The costs of supporting an increasingly expensive and yet unsuccessful military machine became a crushing burden on those very groups who had most benefited from the imperial system in the past: provincial landowners. They, in turn, passed the cost on to their tenant farmers and slaves. As a result, the Empire experienced increasing peasant unrest, sporadic rebellions, and peasant flight. Brigandage, which could mean anything from bandit gangs to serious rebellion, had long been a low-level problem in the Empire. Now, in many uprisings, *coloni* seem to have united with slaves to oppose the increasingly desperate demands of their landlords and owners.

These landowners, especially the members of local councils, were as desperate as their peasants. Pressed by imperial tax collectors to pay their municipal assessments, whether or not they could collect the taxes, many faced ruin. Increasingly, the agents of distant and ineffective Rome were seen by local magnates as enemies more dangerous than any barbarian raiding party. In the European areas of the Empire, which bore the brunt of the violence and disorder, new, breakaway polities began to emerge. Following the inability of the imperial system to prevent the particularly destructive raids of Franks and other barbarians across the Rhone deep into Gaul and even Spain in 259, troops in Gaul raised their commander, Cassius Latinus Postumus, to the imperial purple. He established himself as commander of Gaul, Britain, and parts of Spain, which he and his successors in the so-called "Gallic Empire" ruled until 273.

It would be a mistake to see such breakaway polities as manifestations of developing "national" identities in Gaul or the West. Western aristocrats supported the Gallic Empire because it provided a measure of security and protection to western provinces. It also gave them more immediate access to centers of power and a more direct involvement in political life than had been available in the more centralized imperial system. The Gallic Empire was thus a reasonable response to unreasonable pressures. Nor did support of Postumus and his successors suggest any less dedication to the traditions of *Romanitas*. But if it was not evidence of "Gallic nationalism," it was early evidence that Roman provincials were more concerned with the practical problems of preservation of wealth, security, and status in a local environment than with anachronistic ideals of Roman unity. In a sense, it was a dress rehearsal for the disintegration of the Western Empire in the fifth century.

The Crisis of the Third Century was likewise a crisis in the barbarian world. In the aftermath of the Marcomannan wars, new barbarian "peoples" appeared along the Rhine-Danube frontiers in the course of the third century. Roman authors referred to them collectively as *Germani,* as they would call all of the peoples who appeared on the Rhine frontier regardless of linguistic or other "ethnic" criteria. They further distinguished among these *Germani* those who lived on the lower Rhine as the Franks, or "the Fierce" or "the Free" and those on the upper Rhine as the "Alamanni"— that is, "the People."

Since both designations—*Franci* and *Alamanni*—are Germanic words, the Romans must have learned them either from the members of these groups themselves or from their Germanic-speaking neighbors. Neither name could be found among the "ancient" names of right-Rhine peoples. They were new terms. Since modern historians assumed that "new peoples" had to have come from somewhere, many have sought the origins of the Alamanni in the Elbe region among the Suebi mentioned by Tacitus. They postulated that a portion of the Suebi had migrated to the Roman frontier during the first decades of the third century. More likely, the Alamanni didn't come from anywhere else: They were simply a coalition of indigenous groups, long established on the upper Rhine, who assumed a new collective identity. Similarly, the *Franci* were a confederation of peoples on the lower reaches of the river.

Along the lower Danube, following the Marcomannan wars, another constellation of Germanic, Sarmatic, and even Roman peoples coalesced under the generalship of the Goth Cniva. Behind these constellations on Rome's borders stood still other groups, such as the Saxons beyond the Franks, the Burgundians beyond the Alamanni, and the Vandals beyond the Goths.

Although the barbarians did not cause the crisis of the third century, they certainly added to it. In the 250s, for example, the Gothic King Cniva led his mixed confederation into the province of Dacia, while Gothic pirates attacked the Black Sea coast from the mouth of the Danube. When legions from along the Rhine were shifted east to deal with internal and external problems, barbarians took the opportunity to launch raids across the poorly defended frontier. After Roman troops were withdrawn from the upper reaches of the Rhone and Danube rivers, Alamannic bands (possibly with the approval of some provincial Roman commanders) moved into this so-called Decumanian region. Frankish armies advanced deep into Gaul and even Spain.

Restoration and Transformation

The series of energetic emperors who ended the crisis did so through measures that transformed both the Roman and the barbarian worlds.

The first necessity was subduing the barbarian menace. Emperor Gallienus (253–268) and his successors decisively defeated the Franks and the Alamanni, and the Emperor Aurelian (270–275) crushed the Goths in a series of campaigns that splintered their confederation. Raiding continued sporadically, but the frontiers were essentially secure for another century. Although neither Dacia nor the Decumanian region were entirely retaken by the Empire, imperial measures established a relative security for most of the fourth century.

For some barbarian armies, defeat meant the destruction of their identity as a cohesive social unit. The level of devastation caused by barbarian raids into the Empire paled in comparison with the wasting and slaughter meted out by Roman armies engaged in expeditions across the Rhine or the Danube. A panegyric of the year 310 describes the treatment of the Bructeri after a punitive expedition Constantine led against them: The barbarians were trapped in an area of impenetrable forest and swamp where many were killed, their cattle confiscated, and their villages burned. All the adults were thrown to the beasts in the arena. The children were presumably sold into slavery.

At its most extreme, then, defeat meant the annihilation of a people, the total dissolution of its social and political bonds, and its absorption into the Roman world. In other cases, surviving warriors might be forced into the Roman army. These *dediticii* or *laeti,* following a ritual surrender in which they gave up their weapons and threw themselves on the mercy of their Roman conquerors, were spread throughout the Empire in small units or settled in depopulated areas to provide military service and restore regions devastated by barbarian attacks and taxpayer flight. One such unit of Franks, sent to the shores of the Black Sea, managed a heroic escape, commandeering a ship and making their way across the Mediterranean, through the straits of Gibraltar, and, ultimately, home, but most served out their days in the melting pot of the Roman army.

But if formal surrender, *deditio,* had been a religious ritual of unconditional surrender and annihilation as a people and a society since republican times, the reality had always been at considerable odds with the rhetoric of Roman triumphal ideology. From an equally early time, the conquered and destroyed peoples tended to be restored to some level of identity and autonomy, often with the same political and social elites. Roman mercy (and political imperatives) meant, in reality, the survival of defeated and "annihilated" peoples, reconstituted with a treaty or *foedus* specifying their obligations to the emperor.[5]

However, defeat also meant major changes for those barbarian peoples on the frontiers of the Empire not assimilated into the army or sold into slavery. Unable to support their political and economic systems through raiding, the defeated barbarian military kings found an alternative in service to the Roman Empire. After defeating a Vandal army in 270, the Emperor Aurelian concluded a treaty with the Vandals as federates of the Empire. Similar treaties with Franks and Goths followed before the end of the century. *Foederati* obligated themselves to respect the Empire's frontiers, to provide troops to the imperial army, and, in some cases, to make additional payments in cattle or goods. Barbarian leaders favorable to Rome found that they could reach previously unimaginable heights of power and influence, not by fighting *against* the Empire, but *for* it. Thus, within the barbarian confederations along the *limes,* pro- and anti-Roman factions developed, maintaining a level of tension and disunity within their ranks that was actively fostered by their Roman neighbors.

New forms of relatively stable barbarian polities developed along the Rhine and the Danube as these "new" peoples came to terms with the victorious might of Rome. What sort of self-ascribed identity did members of such groups hold? While we have no direct statements of how barbarians thought of themselves, we do have indirect indications that individuals could simultaneously hold several identities, seeing themselves as part of larger confederations as well as smaller groups. Thus, old "ethnic" names continued to be heard by Roman reporters. The Alamanni settled into the Decumanian region, but maintained a loose and deeply divided sense of identity that only occasionally coalesced, usually under desperate fear of their Roman neighbors.[6] The Alamannic confederation that fought the Emperor Julian in 357, for example, was said to have been led by an uncle and nephew, called "the most outstanding in power before the other kings," five kings of second rank, ten *regales,* and a series of magnates. Although Roman sources dubbed all these leaders *Alamanni,* they also observed that the Alamanni were composed of such groups as the Bucinobantes, the Lentienses, and the Juthungi, under the leadership of their own kings. These subgroups could be termed *gentes,* implying a social and political constitution, or *pagi,* suggesting that their organization was, at least in part, territorial, or, as in the cases of the *Lentienses,* both.

Similarly the early Franks were composed of groups such as the Chamavi, the Chattuarii, the Bructeri, and the Amsivari, and knew numerous *regales* and *duces* who commanded portions of the collectivity and disputed among themselves for primacy. Moreover, Franks could identify not only with these smaller units and with the broader Frankish confederation but with the Roman world as well. A third-century grave marker from Pannonia, erected for a Frankish warrior in Roman service, reads: *Francus ego cives, miles romanus in armis* ("I am a Frank by nationality, but a Roman soldier under arms.")[7] This is no simple statement of barbarian self-identity. Its language and its terminology betray how thoroughly the Roman ideas of citizenship had penetrated this warrior society. That one would be termed a Frankish citizen, seemingly a contradiction in terms, suggests a recognition of the constitutional nature of this Frankish unity. Moreover, by declaring the warrior to be Roman in military service, the inscription emphasizes the new, fundamental reality emerging in the course of the later third century: The Roman army itself was becoming barbarized.

Barbarian Roman warriors could use this dual identity to enhance their position both in the Empire and among their own people. In the late fourth century, for example, the Frankish war leader Arbogast, although in Roman service, used his Roman position to pursue his feud with the Frankish *regales* Marcomer and Sunno in trans-Rhinian territory.

Arbogast was but one of a series of Frankish leaders who could manipulate his dual identities as a Roman and as a Frank. Their rise was actively supported by emperors who needed to find the most economical means to respond to the dual demands on the Roman military caused by internal conflict and by the pressure on

the Persian frontier. Recruitment of barbarians was more economical and effective than raising traditional troops from within
the Empire itself. Constantine I led the way, not only by incorporating Frankish military units into the imperial army as auxiliary
units but also by promoting barbarians, such as the Frank Bonitus,
to high military office. Bonitus was the first in a long series of such
"imperial" Franks. In 355 his son, the thoroughly Romanized Silvanus, who was commander of the Roman garrison at Cologne, was
proclaimed Emperor by his troops. Silvanus wanted to return to
his Frankish people but was assured that, if he did, he would face
death. As it was, he was quickly assassinated by envoys of the Emperor Constantius. Subsequent barbarian commanders, such as
Malarich, Teutomeres, Malllobaudes, Laniogaisus, and Arbogast,
learned the lesson that the imperial title was dangerous. They
avoided usurpation but exercised enormous power within the
Western Empire.

For the most part, these Roman generals maintained their close
ties with members of their peoples outside the Empire. Shortly
after Silvanus's assassination, Franks sacked Cologne, possibly to
avenge his murder. Mallobaudes, who participated in Gratian's victory over the Alamanni in 378, was simultaneously termed *comes
domesticorum* and *rex Francorum* by the Roman historian Ammianus
Marcellinus. Others, such as Arbogast, used their position within
the Empire to attack their enemies across the Rhine. Still, their situation was extremely precarious both within the Empire and outside it. Frequently they were the objects of suspicion by their
Roman competitors, even though they generally were no less reli-
able than Romans in high command. At the same time, as Roman
officials and as adherents of Roman religion—whether Christian
or pagan—they were always targets of anti-Roman factions at
home. Assumption of high Roman command generally meant for-
going the possibility of retaining a position at the head of a barbarian people outside the Empire.

Further to the east, the Gothic confederation with its military kingship splintered under Roman pressure. The Goths living in the easternmost regions, in modern-day Ukraine, accepted the authority of a royal family of the new type that nevertheless claimed ancient and divine legitimacy, while among the western Gothic groups numerous *reiks* (war leaders) shared and disputed an oligarchic control.

By the fourth century, the more eastern Gothic peoples, the Greutungs (the name means roughly "dwellers of the steppes") had absorbed characteristics of the Scyths. In the western regions, the Tervingi ("forest people"), had come under the greatest direct influence of Rome. Both were sedentary agrarian societies, although in the former the military elite was composed primarily of infantry while in the latter horsemen in the tradition of the ancient Scyths formed the core of the army. In the fourth century, the Tervingian Goths had expanded their hegemony over a wide spectrum of peoples with different linguistic, cultic, and cultural traditions.

Settled in agricultural villages and governed by local assemblies of free men, the population of this Gothic confederation was nevertheless subject to the oligarchical authority of Gothic military leaders, themselves under the authority of a super-royal judge or *kindins*. In 332 Constantine and the Tervingian judge Ariaric concluded a treaty or *foedus*. Ariaric's son Aoric was raised in Constantinople and the emperor even erected a statue in the city in honor of the judge. Under Ariaric, Aoric, and his son Athanaric, these western Goths became progressively integrated into the Roman imperial system, providing auxiliary troops to the eastern region of the Empire. One effect of this closer relationship with the Empire was their implication in internal imperial politics and competition. In 365 the usurper Procopius convinced the Tervingians to support him as the representative of the Constantinian dynasty in his opposition to the Emperor Valens. After Procopius's execution, Valens launched a brutal, punitive attack across the Danube that only ended in 369 with a treaty between Athanaric and the emperor.

Religion was a binding force in the Gothic confederation, but the heterogeneous constitution of the confederation created difficulties in maintaining this religious unity. Christians—large numbers of whom were incorporated into the Gothic world from the Crimea during the time of Cniva, while others were carried off in trans-Danubian raids—proved the most difficult religious minority to assimilate, both because of the strong exclusivity of this monotheistic faith and because of the importance of Christianity in the political strategies of the Roman Empire. Gothic Christians represented the spectrum of Christian beliefs, from orthodox (that is, "right-believing" or Catholic) Crimean Goths to the Audaian sect among the Tervingi that confessed the corporeality of God, to various Arian or semi-Arian communities in the Gothic Balkans. The most influential Gothic Christian was Ulfilas (whose Gothic name means Little Wolf), a third-generation Goth of relatively high social standing whose Christian ancestors had been captured in a raid on Cappadocia sometime in the 260s. In the 330s Ulfilas came to Constantinople as part of a delegation, resided in the Empire for some time, and in 341 was consecrated "bishop of the Christians in the Getic land" at the Council of Antioch and sent to the Balkan Goths. Ulfilas's consecration, and his mission to the Goths and other peoples in the Gothic confederation, were part of an imperial Gothic program, which may have precipitated the first persecution of Gothic Christians, in 348 under Aoric, and a second beginning in 369 under Athanaric. During the first persecution, Ulfilas and his followers were exiled to Roman Moesia, where he preached in Gothic, Latin, and Greek to his heterogeneous flock; wrote theological treatises; and translated the Bible, with others, into Gothic. Ulfilas and his followers attempted to steer a middle course between the Catholic and Arian positions on the nature of the divine persons, a position that inevitably resulted in being labeled Arian by future generations of orthodox Christians. In the short run, however, Athanaric's persecution was as little effective as had been the earlier persecution of Christians by Rome. He succeeded only in badly dividing the Gothic peoples, an opportunity seized by the Gothic aristocrat Fritigern, who contacted the Roman Emperor Valens and agreed to become an Arian Christian in return for support against Athanaric.

Internal Transformation

The measures taken to end the crisis had profound effects on those living within the Empire as well as on those living outside imperial control. In an effort to maintain productivity and control over an eroding tax base, occupations across the Empire were made hereditary. Agricultural workers were tied to the estates they worked and were made even more dependent on their estate owners. As the state became ever more burdensome, "brigandage," a euphemism for armed rebellion, became increasingly common. More effective but less violent was simply flight: Peasants fled estates where rents and taxes meant their economic destruction. Areas termed "empty lands" (*agri deserti*) began to appear in the Empire. It is unclear whether these were actually empty areas, depopulated by combinations of warfare and taxation, or simply regions where imperial tax collectors were unable to enforce tax assessments.

Collection of taxes became increasingly burdensome on local city councillors, or *curiales*. Some *curiales* were powerful enough to prosper by acting as enforcers for the imperial tax system, or fisc, through political connections or hired thugs. For others, election to the *curia* was a sentence of financial ruin since *curiales* themselves had to pay all taxes they were unable to collect. Some *curiales* joined peasants in fleeing the imperial burden, retreating from the city to their estates, where, protected by private militias, they could intimidate and resist agents of the fisc. Thus, at both ends of the social spectrum, fiscal demands weakened bonds of loyalty tying local communities to Rome.

The primary agents of central authority with whom local *curiales* came into contact were the tax collectors and the military. Both of these were increasingly alien and threatening to the Roman population as the fourth century progressed. The bureaucratic machine that these funding sources served was also thoroughly restructured and expanded. Under Diocletian, the old mix of civilian and military administration ended in favor of a strict separation of the two. The number of provinces was increased, to reduce the potential for effective separatist action on the part of local governors, and then grouped into large provinces (called dioceses) governed by civilian officers.

The military, too, was restructured in order to better respond to emergencies across the Empire. In place of the ancient system of legions, two units were created. The first line of defense were the *limitanei,* garrison troops stationed on the frontiers and expected to maintain the status quo under normal circumstances. These troops tended to be recruited locally from the frontier populations themselves. Poorly trained and poorly equipped, the *limitanei* relied on massive fortifications constructed along the frontier to repel barbarian raids from across the Rhine or the Danube. Should the frontier troops be overwhelmed, elite, highly mobile, field armies, called *comitatenses,* stationed well behind the lines, could be dispatched to trouble spots.

These administrative and military reorganizations produced a more effective imperial system, but they also had major implications for the social transformation of the Empire. The military structure, in particular, transformed this most Roman of institutions into a powerful mechanism of regionalization and barbarization. Military units stationed along the frontiers, the *limi-*

tanei, turned into a sort of home guard, composed of local recruits, primarily the sons of soldiers. Since these were the least Romanized portions of the Empire's population, these frontier units became increasingly indistinguishable from the barbarians against whom they were to be defending the borders.

The *comitatenses,* too, were increasingly composed of barbarian units recruited from outside the Empire. Expert Gothic horsemen from the steppes of the lower Danube were widely used in the eastern portions of the Empire as federated troops. In some areas of the Empire, the terms "Goth" and "soldier" were used interchangeably. In the West, barbarians from the lower Rhine—Franks—rose to important positions in the military hierarchy. The primary vehicle of Romanization was becoming essentially barbarian.

Concomitant with these fundamental changes in administrative and military composition and function was the profound change in cultural identity introduced by Constantine's conversion. To preserve the religious bonds uniting Roman society in the face of the multiple centrifugal forces of the third century, Diocletian instituted a violent and systematic program of persecution against Christians. The exclusivity of the Christian devotion to their god and their rejection of the age-old rituals that had successfully absorbed virtually all other religious traditions were at the heart of this persecution. In earlier centuries, when Christians had been largely marginal groups, this refusal had resulted in sporadic persecution. However, by the middle of the third century, Christianity had made inroads into the highest levels of Roman society: the senate, the equites, and even the imperial household. That such people would refuse to sacrifice to the *genius,* or spirit, of the emperor was simply intolerable.

In a sense, Constantine and his successors did not reject this line of reasoning. They simply turned it on its head: By legalizing and favoring Christianity, Constantine sought to harness its dynamism for his own imperial program. His successors went still further, replacing by the end of the century the traditional cults of Rome with Christianity and proscribing alternatives as thoroughly as their predecessors had once proscribed followers of Christ.

But this solution introduced problems as profound as those it sought to solve. As Christianity became a state religion, one had to ask about the relationship between *Christianitas* and *Romanitas*. Not everyone living in the Empire was Christian: Were they therefore not fully Roman? Moreover, the Christians were not themselves united. This mattered little in traditional polytheistic religions, but the absolute exclusivity of Christianity demanded total conformity. This while precluding compromise among the different churches and sects, all of whom were convinced that they alone followed the true path of orthodoxy. Finally, the increasing identity of *Romanitas* and *Christianitas* created a dilemma since, by the late third century, there were Christian barbarians and Roman pagans. The conversion of the Empire threatened to lead to greater regionalization and fragmentation of its population.

But even as these issues were being debated, a far greater crisis faced the Romans and their barbarian neighbors: the arrival of the Huns.

Chapter Four

New Barbarians and New Romans

Political and religious tensions between and within the Roman and Barbarian worlds, outlined in Chapter 3, were rendered suddenly irrelevant by the arrival of the Huns. The Huns were a steppe, nomadic confederation under Central Asian leadership, living in the area of the Black Sea in 375. The Huns were like no people ever seen before by Romans or their neighbors: Everything—from their physical appearance to their nomadic lifestyle to their mode of warfare—was foreign and terrible to the Old World. Although they existed as a distinct people for little more than a century, their arrival precipitated major changes, culminating in the creation of barbarian kingdoms within the shell of the western half of the Roman Empire. The result was a dramatic change in the way that both these ruling barbarians and their Roman subjects understood themselves.

The Hunnic confederation was the first of a long series of steppe movements that would terrify China and Europe from the fourth to the fifteenth centuries. Even more than the barbarian peoples of the West, they were able to develop quickly under charismatic leadership from a small core of warriors and expand with explosive force by incorporating defeated nomadic warriors. A later, Turkic inscription describes how this process could take place:

> My father, the khagan, went off with seventeen men. Having heard the news that [he] was marching off, those who were in the towns went up mountains and those who were on mountains came down (from there); thus they gathered and numbered seventy men. Due to the fact that Heaven granted strength, the soldiers of my father, the khagan, were like wolves, and his enemies were like sheep. Having gone on campaigns forward and backward, he gathered together and collected men; and they all numbered seven hundred men. After they had numbered seven hundred men, [my father, the khagan] organized and ordered the people who had lost their state and their khagan, the people who had turned slaves and servants, the people who had lost the Turkish institutions, in accordance with the rules of my ancestors.[1]

This description captures the essence of the process by which nomadic confederations like the Huns and, later, the Mongols could appear so suddenly and grow to enormous importance. A warrior leader manages, through a series of victories, to attract other warriors. A band becomes an army. The army can survive only by continued conquest and incorporation of its victims into the military forces. This conquest and incorporation swells its ranks still further. Then, at a crucial moment, this army is converted to a people through the imposition of legal and institutional structure and, perhaps, claims to a special divine sanction. These may be newly created, but they draw their validity from the claim that they constitute the restoration of an ancient tradition.

Given the vast areas over which such confederations operated, real centralization was always ephemeral, with kinsmen and their close supporters sharing command over portions of the rapidly moving and changing Empire. Except for the short period of the reign of Attila (444–453), the Huns were never a united, centralized people. Rather, they were disparate groups of warrior bands, sharing a common nomadic culture, a military tradition of mounted raiding, and an extraordinary ability to absorb the peoples they conquered into their confederations. Their startling military success was due to their superb cavalry tactics, their proficiency with short, double-reflex bows that allowed them to launch a volley of arrows with deadly accuracy while riding, and their ability to use the steppes and plains of western Asia and Central Europe to appear without warning, inflict tremendous damage, and disappear into the grasslands as quickly as they had come.

Within a generation, these nomadic warrior bands destroyed the barbarian confederations they encountered on the fringes of the Roman Empire. These included, first, the eastern Gothic or Greutung kingdom and then the more western Gothic Tervingian confederation. With the destruction of the authority of Gothic leadership, constituent groups of the old Gothic confederations had to decide whether to join the Hunnic bands or to petition the Emperor to enter and settle in the Roman Empire. Most chose or were forced into the former.

The Hunnic Confederation

For most of the Goths defeated by the Huns, entering the Hunnic confederation was the obvious outcome of their defeat. Although a core of warriors from central Asia provided leadership to the Hunnic armies, in the first generation, the peoples they conquered were easily assimilated without necessarily losing their more particular identities in the confederation. This apparent paradox is important to understanding the fragility and the resilience of ethnic identities in the Migration Period. Good warriors, whether of Gothic, Vandal, Frankish, or even Roman origins, could rise rapidly within the Hunnic hierarchy. Even among the

95

central leadership, this polyethnicity was obvious. One Hunnic leader, Edika, was simultaneously a Hun and a Skirian; after the collapse of the Hunnic Empire, he ruled the short-lived Skirian kingdom north of the Black Sea. The greatest of the Hunnic leaders, Attila, bore a Gothic name (or title): In Gothic, Attila means "Daddy." Gothic, Greek, and Latin were used alongside Hunnic in his court, and his advisors included not only leaders of various barbarian peoples but even former Romans. For a time in the fifth century, the Pannonian aristocrat Orestes—father of the last Roman emperor in the West, Romulus Augustulus—served the Hunnic king. In a famous account of an ambassadorial mission to the court of Attila, an East Roman emissary named Priscus tells of meeting a former Greek merchant who had been captured by the Huns but had distinguished himself in battle and had risen to freedom, had taken a Hunnic wife, and had ultimately found an honored place in Attila's inner circle.[2]

But total assimilation into the Huns was not the fate of every victim of Hunnic conquest. Such assimilation was available to outstanding warriors only. The Hunnic military elite also needed a subservient population to provide it with food as well as to fill the ranks of its army. Peoples such as the Goths served this purpose. Had they been completely assimilated into the Huns, they would have been less useful. Thus, it seems that although the Huns largely destroyed the central political institutions of the peoples they conquered and allowed some of the individuals they captured to "become Huns," they left some indigenous chiefs in charge of their victims. These indigenous chiefs exchanged oaths of loyalty in return for personal and group survival. Thereafter, the Huns looked to these subservient elements as integral units in their confederation both for military service and for the supplies they did not themselves produce.

Such arrangements did not always work out as the Huns hoped. Priscus records that a riot broke out in a Hunnic contingent of the

Roman army in the 460s during an attack by Attila's son Dengizich because of this Hunnic practice. A Hunnic commander reminded the Gothic chiefs in the army that the Huns "have no concern for agriculture, but, like wolves, attack and steal the Goths' food supplies, with the result that the latter remain in the position of servants and themselves suffer food shortages."[3] Stung by the memory of this treatment, the Goths turned on the Huns among them and killed them.

Thus, while in time some conquered groups may have lost their identity entirely, throughout the history of the Huns, Romans noted the tendency of individuals, bands, and larger groups to break off and attempt to escape into the safety of Roman territory. Such groups were not necessarily whole "peoples" or even victims of Hunnic conquest. They included small bands, individuals, and even Huns who had a falling out with their own leaders. Such losses were a threat to Hunnic control, as evidenced by Attila's regular demands that refugees be returned as part of any treaty. The leaders of these forcibly returned groups faced certain death by crucifixion or empaling.

In order to maintain the unity of this heterogeneous Hunnic confederation, its chieftains needed a constant flow of treasure, the principal source of which was from raiding the Empire or serving the emperor against its other enemies in return for annual subsidies. Initially, raids on the Illyrian and Thracian borders of the Empire provided the bulk of the booty. The spoils from such raids were just the beginning, since emperors provided annual subsidies to Hunnic commanders in order to prevent further incursions. Thus, it is clear that the ability to conduct successful military operations was essential for the survival of Hunnic leaders.

During the first decades of the Hunnic confederation, leadership was shared by members of a royal family, but in 444 Attila eliminated his brother Bleda after Hunnic successes began to falter and unified the Huns under his command. Under Attila, annual payments by the Emperor Theodosius II increased from 350 to 700 pounds of gold, and eventually to 2,100 pounds of gold, an enormous amount to the barbarians but not a devastating burden on the Empire. Theodosius apparently found it cheaper to pay off Attila than to raise an army to defend against Hunnic raids. Moreover, the Huns proved useful allies both outside the Empire and, when needed, within it as well.

After the death of Theodosius II in 450, his successor Marcian refused to continue the preferential treatment accorded to the Huns. With this source of funding gone, Attila apparently considered himself too weak to extract adequate booty by raiding the Eastern Empire and turned his attention to the Western Empire of Valentinian III. He led his armies west in two long raids. The first in 451 reached far into Gaul before being stopped at the battle of the Catalaunian Plains between Troyes and Châlons-sur-Marne. There Attila's army—probably composed primarily of subject Germanic peoples from the western areas of his control, such as Suevi, Franks, and Burgundians in addition to Gepids, Goths, and descendants of Central Asian Huns—was stopped by an equally heterogeneous army of Goths, Franks, Bretons, Sarmats, Burgundians, Saxons, Alans, and Romans under the command of the patrician Aetius, an old friend and former ally of the Huns. In all probability, the two armies were virtually indistinguishable to an uninformed observer.

The second raid came the following year when Attila led another army into Italy. Again, in keeping with Hunnic priorities, the expedition was primarily undertaken for pillage, not for lasting political objectives, and ended near Verona when, weakened by disease and far from their accustomed terrain, they turned back. Only later was their reversal attributed to the efforts of Pope Leo I. In reality, they were probably all too ready to return to the steppe.

The essential fragility of an Empire such as Attila's was demonstrated by its rapid disintegration following his death. Steppe Empires built on victory could not endure defeat. A separatist coalition under the leadership of the Gepid Ardaric revolted against Attila's sons. The rebels were victorious and the defeat of Attila's sons led to the splintering of the old confederation and new processes of ethnogenesis. In addition to the Gepid alliance, there emerged the Rugii, the Skiri, and the Sarmatians along the Danube, and the Ostrogoths, who gathered the remnants of the Greutungs and entered Roman service as *foederati*. Some of Attila's sons continued to lead splinter groups, some apparently returning to southern Russia, others entering Roman service within the Roman military aristocracy. Within a few generations, they and their followers had become Ostrogoths, Gepids, or Bulgars.

Barbarian Ethnogenesis within the Empire

A different fate met those barbarians who fled the Hunnic onslaught in 375. While the majority of the Greutungs and Alans were absorbed into the new Hunnic confederation, a minority, augmented by deserting Huns, fled toward the *limes*. So, too, did most of the Tervingi, who abandoned Athanaric's leadership and fled with Fritigern across the Danube. The flight of the Tervingi into the Empire set in motion a decisive transformation in the identity of Fritigern's followers. From the Roman perspective, they were but *dediticii*, defeated enemies, received into the Empire under the command of Roman officers. They were allowed to settle in Thrace, where they were expected to support themselves through agriculture while supplying troops to the military. The reality was that, in quality and quantity, the Tervingian refugees' situation was very different from that of earlier *dediticii*. First, these Goths were far more numerous than earlier barbarian bands allowed into the Empire, overwhelming the Roman administrative abilities. Second, the Romans did not force them to surrender their arms, as was the usual practice. When Roman mistreatment and Gothic hunger pushed the refugees to armed resistance, the result was a series of Gothic victories. Soon the refugee cavalry of the Greutungs, the Alans, and the Huns joined the Tervingi, as did Gothic units already in the Roman army, Thracian miners, barbarian slaves, and the poor. The Gothic victories culminated in 378 with the annihilation of the imperial army and the death of Valens at Adrianople.

After Adrianople, Rome could no longer treat these Goths as defeated and subjugated. In a treaty concluded in 382, they were recognized as a federated people but were allowed to settle between the Danube and the Balkan mountains with their own governors, creating, in effect, a state within a state. Tax revenues traditionally collected for the support of the military were redirected to the support of the barbarians. In return, the barbarians were required to provide military support to the Empire, but they did so under their own commanders, who were subordinate to Roman generals.

At the same time, the unprecedented success of the Tervingians and their allies led to a fundamental transformation of this disparate band of refugees into the Visigoths, a new people with a new cultural and political identity. The Visigoths quickly adapted the mounted tactics used so effectively by the Greutungs, the Alans, and the Huns in their campaigns against Valens, in effect transforming themselves into a highly mobile cavalry in the steppe tradition.

Fritigern and most of his followers had been Arian Christians, a choice probably related to his initial attempts to please the Emperor Valens. After Adrianople, this Arian faith became an integral part of Visigothic self-identity—a way of distinguishing this new people from the majority of orthodox Christians within the Empire.

For the next generation, the Visigoths struggled to maintain themselves as a Gothic confederation and simultaneously as a Roman army. Their king, Alaric, who claimed membership in the royal clan of the Balths, sought recognition and payments both as the ruler of a federated people and as a high-ranking general or *magister militum* in imperial service with de facto command of the civilian and military bureaucracies in the regions under his authority. He pursued both these goals through alternate service to and expeditions against the Eastern and Western emperors and their imperial barbarian commanders.

In his insistence on his dual role, Alaric stood in contrast to another, older model of imperial barbarian embodied by Stilicho, the supreme military commander in the West and intermittently his commander, ally, and bitter enemy. Stilicho was of Vandal origins, but he, like pagan Frankish and Alamannic Roman commanders before him, had abandoned his ties to the people of his birth. He was a Roman citizen, an orthodox Catholic, and operated entirely within the Roman tradition, alternately serving and manipulating both the imperial family as guardian and later father-in-law of the Emperor Honorius and barbarian federates such as Alaric. Stilicho's path proved fatal when he was unable to maintain the integrity of the Rhine and Danubian *limes*. On the last day of the year in 406, bands of Vandals, Suebi, and Alans crossed the Upper Rhine to ravage Gaul and penetrate as far as Spain unhindered. Around the same time, Gothic bands fleeing the Huns invaded Italy from Pannonia. In spite of Stilicho's ultimate success in defeating the Gothic invaders, these twin disasters played into his enemies' hands. In 408 he was deposed and executed on orders given by his son-in-law. Following his death, thousands of other assimilated barbarians living in Italy were likewise slaughtered. By the beginning of the fifth century, Roman political and civic identity was no longer sufficient for political survival in the West.

Surviving barbarians in Italy rallied behind Alaric, whose dual role as barbarian king and Roman commander offered a more fruitful and ultimately durable model of identity. His efforts to win recognition and payments to support his followers prompted his invasion of Italy in 408. Botched negotiations led, after numerous feints, to the capture and pillage of Rome on August 24–26, 410, an event that sent shock waves throughout the Empire. Although his subsequent attempt to lead his people to the fertile lands of Africa failed, and he died in southern Italy, Alaric had established an enduring form of barbarian-Roman polity.

Alaric's successor and brother-in-law Athaulf led the Goths out of Italy and into Gaul. Like other barbarian commanders, he longed for acceptance and assimilation into the Roman imperial elite. At Narbonne in the year 414, he married a sister of the Emperor Honorius, Galla Placidia, who had been taken hostage in Rome, in the hope of entering the imperial family of Theodosius. The chimera of winning political advantage through marriage into the imperial family (even if essentially a thinly veiled rape) was one that would recur over the next century; Attila made claims to the throne through marriage to Honoria, the sister of Valentinian III, and the Vandal pretender Huneric married his hostage Eudocia, Valentinian's daughter, with similar designs. None of these attempts accomplished either peace or parity with the Roman Empire. The Empire after all, unlike a barbarian king's army, could not be inherited.

Athaulf fell to an assassin and, after futile attempts first to reenter Italy and then to reach North Africa, his successors accepted a new treaty with the mandate to clear Spain of provincial rebels as well as of Vandals and Alans. Following their return to Toulouse in 418, the Visigoths began the form of political and social organization that would characterize their kingdom and those of other federated barbarians, notably the Burgundians and the Ostrogoths.

The barbarians, whatever their original ethnic origins, formed a small but powerful military minority within a much larger Roman population. As mounted warriors, they tended to settle on strategic border areas of their territories or in the political capitals. These barbarian armies were supported by assigning to them a portion of traditional tax revenues that had gone to the imperial fisc, thus minimizing the burden of the barbarian occupation on the landowning Roman aristocracy and keeping these professional warriors free for military service. Collection and distribution of these taxes remained in the hands of the municipal office holders, or *curiales*, likewise minimizing the effects on the landowning aristocracy that monopolized these offices. At least this seems to have been the arrangement with the Visigoth army in 418, the Burgundians in 443, and the Ostrogoths in Italy during the 490s. In other cases, such as that of a group of Alans settled around Valence in 440, the barbarians were assigned tax debts no longer being collected by imperial officials. Through these tax shares, barbarian kings were able to provide for their followers without forcing these followers to disperse into the countryside in order to supervise the management of estates.

In the tradition of Alaric, barbarian kings were not only commanders of their people, but simultaneously high-ranking Roman officials (*magister militum, patricius,* etc.). They exercised supreme authority over the civilian administrative system in their territory, effectively governing the two elements of the Roman state that had been, since the time of Diocletian, separate.

From the perspective of restive Roman provincial landowners, the presence of the barbarians was a mixed blessing. Barbarian armies were much less expensive to maintain and, apparently, less disruptive of agriculture than a standing army of provincials. Likewise, barbarian commanders may have been more responsive to local interests and more willing to negotiate with the local aristocracy than their Roman counterparts.

Roman Provincials in the Fifth and Sixth Centuries

We have seen that, already in the third century, members of the provincial aristocracy in the West were prepared to place their local interests above an ephemeral ideal of imperial unity. In the fourth and fifth centuries, this tendency had become even more marked. At the top of society, among the wealthy provincial aristocracy, a rediscovery, or perhaps an invention, of a feeling of connection to an ancient, pre-Roman past, emerged as a powerful source of regional self-perception. Meanwhile, at the bottom of society, among the peasantry, desperate people were prepared to become rebels or barbarians in order to survive.

The cultivation of a provincial identity is most obvious in the literature composed in Gaul in the fourth century through the early sixth century. In letters and poetry, provincials such as Ausonius (ca. 310–395)—a doctor's son from Bordeaux who became the tutor for the future emperor Gratian and eventually rose to the position of consul—and Sidonius (ca. 430–484)—an aristocrat from Lyon—expressed their deepest feelings not for Rome, or even for Gaul, but for their particular cities.[4] Ausonius sings the praises of his beloved Bordeaux while Sidonius focuses on the Auvergne. Across Gaul, expressions of love for the *patria* focused not on Rome or even some chimeric "Gaul," beloved of French nationalist historians, but, rather, on Marseille, Narbonne, Trier, Lyon, or other *civitates*. Not that these aristocrats necessarily identified themselves in conflict with Rome. In the words of Ausonius:

> This [Bordeaux] is my own country; but Rome stands above countries. I love Bordeaux, Rome I venerate; in this I am a citizen, in both a consul; here was my cradle, there my curial [consular] chair.[5]

In the same sense that a warrior could be a Frank and a Roman, so, too, could a consul be a Bordelais and a Roman. The two identities were not mutually incompatible, but circumstances could dictate which prevailed over the other.

At the same time that gentlemen-poets sang the glories of their *patriae,* their cities, they began to resurrect the pre-Roman names of Gallic tribes that had occupied this region at the time of the caesar's conquest. Some might be tempted to see this as strong evidence of the survival of pre-Roman tribal sentiment across three centuries. This is improbable. Much more likely, it is an intentional literary archaizing, a romantic appeal to ancient tradition. If Ausonius states that his maternal grandfather sprang from the *gens Haedua*[6] and that his maternal grandmother had been a Tarbellian, or, indeed, that he himself was of the Viviscuan *gens,* this is less evidence of a vigorous survival of Gallic tribalism than of archaizing regionalism.

This regionalism continued to grow in strength over the next century. It is evident in the emergence of a whole list of cognomina derived from tribal names in Late Antiquity.[7] These included, among many others, "Allobrogicinus" from the Allobroges, "Arvernicus" from the Arverni, "Morinus" from the Morini, "Remus" from the Remi, and "Trever" from the Treveri. These same tribal names likewise emerged as the vernacular names for Roman cities founded in their regions. Thus, *Lutectia Parisiorum* failed to emerge in the vernacular as *Lutèce,* but, rather, as *Paris.*

This literary nostalgia for an ancient past, however artificial it might have been in terms of pre-Roman tribal identity, was a very real indication of a growing regionalism. Significantly, it was a regionalism that willingly identified sophisticated aristocrats with the kinds of "tribal" (we might say "gentile") characteristics traditionally imputed by Greco-Roman ethnographers to barbarians. Ausonius describes his mother as of "mixed blood" (*sanguine mixto*) because of her parents' origins in different *gentes.* Sidonius analyzes the ancestry of one Lupus, descended on his father's side from the

Nitiobroges, and on that of his mother's from the Vesunnici.[8] As identity fell back on local cities, it looked not to the Roman administrative creation for its inspiration so much as to the pre-Roman tribal or gentile tradition. If the provincial aristocracy could be so categorized and analyzed, then they could be seen as no different from the barbarians who increasingly dominated the political and military scene.

At the other end of the social spectrum, too, slaves, freedpersons, *coloni,* and small landholders were experimenting with new identities. Little evidence suggests that they discovered pre-Roman tribal roots and forged a sense of solidarity with regional aristocratic landowners so enamored of their putative tribal origins. Rather, they sought refuge either with the traditional bandits endemic to the Roman world, or with the barbarian military.

In the fifth century, bands of so-called *bagaudae* threatened Roman administration and fiscal operations in southern Gaul and Spain. The name, which probably has its origin in the Celtic word for war, had been applied to rural rebels since the third century. These fifth-century *bagaudae,* unlike earlier bandits, included a cross-section of the provincial population who felt persecuted or abandoned by the Empire and focused their hatred both on the agents of the fisc and the great landowners. Like barbarian armies, the *bagaudae* roamed the countryside, at times banding together to protect their region from barbarian raids in the absence of Roman troops, and at other times joining forces with barbarian armies to lay siege to cities, thoroughly terrifying the elites. According to one report, in the early fifth century the *bagaudae* of Amorica first expelled the barbarian invaders and then the Roman magistrates. The region was only pacified in 417.[9]

Bagaudae, for all the fear they instilled in their betters, failed to create long-lasting independent political and corporate identities. They were, without exception, crushed by imperial authority, often with the assistance of barbarian federates. Thus, barbarian feder-

landowners as well as that of the African orthodox Church, which had a long tradition of political activism developed during decades of opposition to Donatist schismatics. Many of the landowning aristocracy fled or were exiled, as were the Catholic bishops, who only returned in the 520s. Vandal kings eventually won imperial recognition, but even then their rule remained tenuous. Hated and isolated from the rest of the population, the Vandals were an unexpectedly easy prey for conquest when the Emperor Justinian sent an invading army to North Africa in 533. Two decisive battles broke the kingdom, and the remaining Vandals were deported and dissolved into various federated barbarian armies in the eastern Mediterranean. Within less than a decade, the Vandals had entirely disappeared.

The Ostrogothic kingdom in Italy, established by Theodoric the Great in the 490s, began with greater prospects but likewise fell to Byzantine reconquest. The Ostrogoths emerged from the ruins of the Hunnic Empire as one of the Germanic factions, alternatively allying with and fighting against the eastern Empire. In 484, Theodoric, who claimed descent from the pre-Hunnic royal Amal family, united a number of these groups under his command. Four years later, he led a polyethnic army into Italy on behalf of the Emperor Zeno against Odovacer, a barbarian commander, who had made himself master of Italy. Odovacer was an old-fashioned barbarian Roman commander—a king without a people. Like Stilicho before him, Odovacer governed Italy and commanded an army composed of the remnants of Roman regular and federate troops. He was no match for Theodoric and his Goths. In 493 Theodoric gained control of the peninsula, eliminated Odovacer, and took over the Roman fiscal and administrative system.

Theodoric sought to transform his heterogeneous, mobile barbarian army into a stable, settled, Gothic people capable of peaceful co-existence within Roman Italy. His goal for his Gothic following was "civility" (*civilitas*); that is, to convince them to adopt

ates became useful not only to protect the borders of the Empire from outside invaders but also to protect it from within. Not long after the Visigoths sacked Rome, they were sent into southern Gaul to suppress the *bagaudae*. In the 430s it was the Huns who were sent to crush the *bagaudae* south of the Loire.

Barbarians were no more inclined to tolerate provincial uprisings of *bagaudae* than were imperial officials. After all, barbarian federates, too, depended on regular tax collection for their support. Frequently, barbarians made common cause with imperial officials and the senatorial aristocracy of the threatened provinces. However, barbarian armies remained fluid bands of warriors and, as such, attracted discontented and desperate provincials as strongly as did the bands of rebels. Some people apparently even went from one group to the other, seeking in *bagaudae* and barbarians alternatives to their plight. According to a fifth-century chronicle, a physician, Eudoxius, first joined the *bagaudae* and then later the Huns.[10] In the mid–fifth century, the Christian moralist Salvian argued that ordinary provincials in Spain and Gaul found more security in identifying with the barbarians than with the Empire:

> They (the poorest Romans) seek among the barbarians Roman humanitarianism because they cannot bear the inhumane barbarity they find among the Romans. . . . Thus they go over either to the Goths or to the *bagaudae*, or to other barbarians everywhere in power . . . And thus the name of Roman citizen, once not only highly esteemed but purchased at a great price, now is instead refused and shunned.[11]

Thus, at the same time that Roman provincial elites were cultivating an identity that connected them with long-vanished Gallic tribes, provincial masses, feeling abandoned by the Empire and exploited by the aristocracy, sought new identities among the barbarian invaders and federates. Neither group viewed simply being Roman as particularly useful.

New Land and New Identity

The settlement of barbarian armies within the western half of the Empire precipitated further changes in social and ethnic identity. A barbarian people on the march was one thing—it was a porous army, readily recruiting soldiers of all backgrounds. A barbarian kingdom was something else—it sought to create boundaries between itself and the majority of the local population. Once established in former Roman provinces, barbarian kings began the attempt to transform the culturally disparate members of their armies into a unified people with a common law and a common sense of identity. At the same time, rather than recruiting new members, they attempted to maintain a certain distance from the majority Roman population in their kingdoms.

The identity they offered the members of their "people" was drawn from vague family traditions reinterpreted and transformed by the new situations in which they found themselves. In particular, successful rulers of these new kingdoms claimed illustrious descent from ancient royal or noble families. This was true whether or not these claims were legitimate and, indeed, whether or not these families had ever actually commanded sizable barbarian armies in the past. For the Visigoths, the Balth family provided the center of this tradition. For the Vandals, it was the Hasdings; for the Ostrogoths, the Amals. Successful kings projected their family's imagined past onto the people as a whole, providing a common sense of origin to be shared by the whole of the military elite while suppressing alternative claims to legitimate authority.

To a lesser extent, barbarian kings likewise used religion to found a common identity. The Gothic royal families, like those of the Vandals, the Burgundians, and other peoples, were mostly Arian, and this heterodox version of Christian faith became closely identified with the king and his people. Arianism was neither a proselytizing faith nor a persecuting one. At the most, Arians demanded the use of one or more churches for their worship. Otherwise, orthodox Christianity was not proscribed or persecuted. The exception appears to have been the Vandal kingdom of North Africa, but even here the persecutions and confiscations directed against the orthodox Church seemed to have more to do with confiscation of land and repression of political opponents than doctrinal differences.

Barbarian kings also relied on legal tradition to forge a new identity for their peoples. Nothing is known about the earliest phases of barbarian law codes: The earliest, the Visigothic Code of Euric, dates from circa 470–480. Although, in general, barbarian law codes appear to stand in sharp contrast to Roman law—with its system of tariffs for offenses (*wergeld*), the use of oaths, and formal oral procedure—such traditions may not have been much different from local vulgar legal practice in large areas of the west by the fifth century. These laws sought to delineate rights and responsibilities of barbarians and Romans. They were territorial laws, intended to be applied to barbarians and Romans alike, although not to the exclusion of other vulgar Roman legal traditions, alive in the territories granted the barbarian armies.

Royal efforts to forge new and enduring ethnic and political identities for their peoples within these kingdoms met with varying degrees of success. The gap between the barbarian military and political minority on the one hand and the Roman population on the other remained most sharply divided in Vandal Africa. The Vandals, unlike most of the other barbarian peoples within the Empire, had carved out a kingdom without benefit of a treaty with the Empire and had confiscated property on a wide scale. These confiscations won for them the enduring hatred of aristocratic

Roman principles of the rule of law and Roman traditions of tolerance and consensus in civic society, which they were to protect by their military valor. Nevertheless, he intended to maintain Goths and Romans as separate communities—one military, one civilian—living in mutual dependence under his supreme authority. Thus, Theodoric pursued what has been called an "ethnographic ideology" that distinguished between soldiers (Goths) and civilians (Romans) or, one might almost say, between soldiers and the taxpayers who supported them.[12] The two *nationes,* according to this ideology, existed together in one *populus,* governed by law, not arms, and united in mutual charity.

Nevertheless, Theodoric's rule rested on the reality of Gothic military power. Although Theodoric received the loyal support of Roman administrators and even the close advisors of Odovacar, such as the Senator Cassiodorus, like other barbarian kings, he sought to strengthen the Gothic element of his rule by appointing his personal agents, or *comites,* to supervise and intervene throughout the Roman bureaucracy. He likewise privileged the Arian Church as the "church of the law of the Goths," but he saw to it that it remained a minority church, which he prohibited from proselytizing among the orthodox majority.

In his emphasis on the Gothic element of his rule, both within and outside of Italy, Theodoric relied increasingly on his claim to descend from the legendary royal Amal family, although the validity of these claims, or even of the pre-eminence of this family in the past, cannot be ascertained. Particularly in dealing with external *gentes,* such as the Burgundians, the Visigoths, the Franks, and the Thuringians, it was not *civilitas* or *Romanitas* but the common kinship among the royal families—either by common descent, marriage alliance, or adoption—that he emphasized to cultivate a sense of unity. Moreover, he claimed that the glory of Amal blood placed him above these other, lesser kings.[13] As his reign progressed, such appeals to Amal tradition become more frequent in his internal propaganda, and returned with force in the reign of his grandson Athalaric.

Theodoric's attempt to bring about a new Gothic ethnogenesis, based on Arian faith and Amal descent, failed. The boundaries between Ostrogothic warrior and Roman civilian blurred, as many barbarians became landowners increasingly tied to the same economic and regional concerns as their Roman neighbors. The next generation of Goths, educated in the traditions of the Roman elite, felt even further from the warrior culture designated for them. At the same time, some Romans rose in the ranks of the military and adopted Gothic tradition even to the extent of learning the Gothic language and marrying Gothic women. The patricius Cyprian, for example, went so far as to educate his children in the Gothic style, giving them military training and even having them learn the Gothic language.[14] During the reign of Athalaric, Romans even acquired the right to be judged before the count of the Goths if both Roman parties consented, an intolerable confusion of the principle of separation as developed under Theodoric.[15]

In reaction to this increasing blurring of Gothic distinctiveness, an anti-Roman reaction set in among members of the military, who were concerned about the rapid Romanization of many in their ranks. Tensions mounted following Theodoric's death and culminated in the murder of his daughter Amalasuntha in 535. The Emperor Justinian took the murder as an excuse to refuse to recognize the legitimacy of the Gothic king, Theodehad, Theodoric's nephew, and to invade Italy. Unlike the reconquest of Africa, however, which was accomplished in two battles, this war lasted almost two decades and devastated Italy more profoundly than had all of the barbarian invasions of the previous two centuries. However, the ultimate fate of the Ostrogoths in Italy was similar to that of the Vandals of North Africa. The Ostrogoths ceased to exist as a polity and vanished entirely.

However, it was not only the Ostrogoths who disappeared in the bloodbath of the reconquest. The "Romans"—in the sense of the great senatorial families who had cooperated with Theodoric's attempt at forging a kingdom based on Roman *civilitas* and Gothic arms—perished as well. The identities of both had become so complex and intertwined that the reconquest by Justinian's armies was as fatal to the former as to the latter. Neither the "Romans," in the sense of the imperial troops from Constantinople, nor the Goths trusted them. During the siege of Rome in 537, for example, the Roman commander Belasarius deposed Pope Silverius out of fear that he was negotiating treasonably with the Goths. Belasarius exiled him, along with a number of the most distinguished senators, including Flavius Maximus, a descendant of an emperor, because he had previously married a Gothic princess. During this siege the Gothic king Witigis became so exasperated that he executed all of the senators he had been holding as hostages in Ravenna.[16] In 552, following a major Gothic defeat at the battle of Busta Gallorum, the retreating Goths slaughtered all the Romans they met and King Teja ordered the death of all the senators in Campania, including Flavius Maximus, exiled by the suspicious Belasarius. Shortly thereafter, Teja massacred 300 Roman children Totila had selected as hostages.[17] Equally suspect to Empire and barbarian alike, the ancient Roman aristocracy in Italy never again reappeared as a significant player on the Italian stage.

In Gaul, the Gothic kingdom of Toulouse and the Burgundian kingdom met similar fates. Both continued to serve as federates, participating, for example, in the defeat of the Huns in the battle of the Catalaunian Plains at which Attila was defeated. They likewise profited from imperial weakness to expand their territories. The Goths eventually expanded their control north to the Loire and south through Spain, while the Burgundians expanded east until being driven back by the Gepids. Still, the Visigoths remained a small Arian minority and disappeared in Gaul after a single defeat at the hands of the Franks in 507. The Burgundians rapidly lost any cultural, religious, or genealogical identity they may ever have had, and, by the sixth century, *Burgundian* seems to have meant little more than the holder of lands that had originally been the military allotments divided among the barbarians.

Northern Barbarian Ethnogenesis

The type of barbarian polity pioneered by the Visigoths and largely adopted by the Vandals and Ostrogoths—that is, the creation and maintenance of two communities, one orthodox, Roman, and civilian; the other Arian, barbarian, and military, under the unified command of a barbarian king holding an imperial commission—ended in failure. More enduring were the kind of kingdoms created by the Franks in northern Gaul as well as by the petty kings of Britain, in which Roman and barbarian distinctions rapidly disappeared. The reasons for these successes are several. In part, their distance from the core of the Byzantine world meant that by the early fifth century they were already considered expendable by the Empire and in the sixth they lay beyond the reach of Justinian's reconquest. In part, too, the transformation of Roman civil administration may have been sufficiently advanced that little remained for barbarian kings to absorb. In the case of the Franks, Roman civil administration seems to have survived only at the level of individual *civitates*. In the case of Britain, not even the bureaucratic system at the local level appears to have survived for the new rulers to incorporate into their government. Finally, the barbarians themselves were different. Although the Franks and the Saxons initially served as federates of the Empire, they had no direct experience of the Mediterranean world of Constantinople or even Italy. They, like the provincial Romans they absorbed, were far removed from the cultural and administrative traditions of a Theodoric or a Cassiodorus. The results were a simpler, but, in the long run more thorough, transformation of these peoples into new social and cultural forms.

In the early fifth century, Britain and northern Gaul, long peripheral to the concerns of Ravenna and Constantinople, were forced to look to their own protection and organization. In both areas, regional affinities began to take precedence over wider Roman organization, and new political constellations of Roman, Celtic, and Germanic elements emerged. In Britain, the Roman centralized government faded away, to be replaced by a plethora of small, mutually hostile kingdoms. During the later fifth century and the early sixth century, Germanic federates, drawn from the Saxons, the Frisians, the Franks, and other coastal regions, came to dominate many of these kingdoms, particularly in the Southeast. Although migration from the coastal regions of the continent was significant, particularly in the sixth century, the frequent appearance of Celtic names in the genealogies of early "Anglo-Saxon" kingdoms, as well as the survival of Christian communities within these kingdoms, indicates that the Anglo-Saxon ethnogenesis stemmed from the gradual fusion of indigenous populations with various new arrivals under the political leadership of families that, in time, came to regard themselves as descendants of mythical Germanic heroes. Indeed, most Anglo-Saxon royal genealogies traced their ancestry back to the war god Woden or even to "god" himself, Géat/Gaut.

Frankish society was the result of a similar fusion that took place in the northern portions of Gaul, those most removed from Mediterranean concerns. In the course of the fifth century, a series of rival kingdoms emerged from the ruins of Roman provincial administration, each headed by a warlord or king. Some of these leaders were Frankish kings who commanded largely barbarian units with ties on both sides of the Rhine. Others were mem-

115

bers of the Gallo-Roman aristocracy and drew support from mixed Roman provincial and barbarian armies. Among the former were members of the Merovingian family, who commanded barbarian troops descended from Salian Franks who probably settled within the Empire in the late fourth century. Ethnic affiliation was much less significant in these constellations than political expediency: The followers of the Frankish King Childeric, who had grown wealthy and powerful in the service of the Empire, for example, seem to have been quite willing to transfer their allegiance to Roman warlord-aristocrats when it suited their interests.

Beginning in 486, Childeric's son Clovis expanded his power from his father's kingdom, centered around Tournai, south and east. He captured Soissons, the administrative center of Belgica Secunda, temporarily dominated the Thuringians, and defeated the Alamanni between 496 and 506. In 507 he defeated and killed the Visigothic King Alaric II and began a process of conquering the Visigothic kingdom north of the Pyrenees. None of his conquests appear to have been based on a commission or treaty with Constantinople, but, following his victory over Alaric II, emissaries of Emperor Anastasius granted him some form of imperial recognition, probably an honorary consulship. He spent his final years until his death around 511 eliminating other Frankish kings and rival members of his own family who ruled kingdoms similar to that of his father in Cologne, Cambrai, and elsewhere.

Ethnogenesis proceeded differently in Clovis's Frankish kingdom than it did in Ostrogothic Italy or Visigothic Aquitaine. He did not base his conquests on a direct imperial mandate nor did he attempt to create the sort of dual society erected by an earlier generation of barbarian kings. Salian Franks had long been in Gaul, deeply involved in imperial and regional political struggles for generations. Clovis's authority had been recognized by representatives of the Gallo-Roman aristocracy, such as Bishop Remegius of Rheims, since the death of his father in 486 and long before his conversion to Christianity. Thus, his absorption of rival power centers caused much less dramatic change than had those of earlier barbarian kings. He certainly took over the remnants of Roman civil administration, but these, as we have seen, did not extend above the level of individual *civitates.*

Moreover, there is little evidence that the Franks had or attempted to create as strong and distinct a sense of identity vis-à-vis the Roman population, as had Theodoric or other Gothic commanders. Clovis's family apparently claimed some semi-divine descent and counted a minotaurlike beast among its ancestors, but no Frankish genealogical lore could rival the generations of heroes and gods in Gothic tradition. Rather than claiming ancient traditions separate from Rome, the Franks emphasized their commonalities: Already in the sixth century, the Franks may have claimed Trojan ancestry, thus connecting themselves genealogically to their Roman neighbors.

Franks were prepared not only to share common descent with Romans but common religion as well. Prior to the sixth century, some Franks had been Christian, whether Arian or orthodox, while others, including Clovis's family, had retained a pagan religious tradition. Clovis probably flirted with the Arianism of his powerful neighbor Theodoric, but ultimately accepted orthodox baptism, although exactly when this event took place remains open to debate.

United by a common religion and a common legend of origin, nothing prevented Clovis's Franks and the Roman provincials of his kingdom from forging a common identity. This they did with considerable rapidity. Within only a few generations, the population north of the Loire had become uniformly Frankish and, while Roman legal traditions persisted in the south and Burgundian and Roman legal status endured in the old Burgundian kingdom conquered by Clovis's sons in the 530s, these differing legal traditions did not constitute the basis for a separate social or political iden-

117

tity. The great strength of the Frankish synthesis was the creation of a unified society, drawing on the legacies of Roman and barbarian traditions.

Conclusion: Old Names and New Peoples

The fourth and fifth centuries saw fundamental changes in the European social and political fabric. In the process, great confederations like those of the Goths disappeared, to re-emerge transformed into kingdoms in Italy and Gaul. Others like the Hunnic Empire or the Vandal kingdom seemed to spring from nowhere, only to vanish utterly in a few generations. Still other, previously obscure peoples, such as the Angles and the Franks, emerged to create enduring polities. But whether enduring or ephemeral, the social realities behind these ethnic names underwent rapid and radical transformation in every case. Whatever a Goth was in the third-century kingdom of Cniva, the reality of a Goth in sixth-century Spain was far different, in language, religion, political and social organization, even ancestry. The Franks defeated by Emperor Julian in the fourth century and those who followed Clovis into battle in the sixth century were likewise almost immeasurably distant from each other in every possible way. The same was true of the Romans, whose transformation was no less dramatic in the same period. With the constant shifting of allegiances, intermarriages, transformations, and appropriations, it appears that all that remained constant were names, and these were vessels that could hold different contents at different times.

Names were renewable resources; they held the potential to convince people of continuity, even if radical discontinuity was the lived reality. Old names, whether of ancient peoples like the Goths or Suebi or of illustrious families such as the Amals, could be reclaimed, applied to new circumstances, and used as rallying cries for new powers. Alternatively, names of small, relatively unimportant groups might be expanded with enormous power. The Franks were the most significant of these. In the third century, they were among the least significant of Rome's enemies. By the sixth century, the name *Frank* had eclipsed not only that of *Goth, Vandal,* and *Sueb,* but of *Roman* itself in much of the West.

~~~~~~~

The Last Barbarians?

The creation of new territorial kingdoms in the former Roman Empire in the course of the sixth century changed the nature both of the peoples who gave their names to these regional polities and that of the "new" barbarians who moved into the frontier areas abandoned by these groups. In this chapter we will examine how the establishment in Gaul, Italy, Spain, the Balkans, and even Britain, meant a blurring of the lines between Roman and barbarian, when not abolishing them altogether.

Amalgamation within the Western Kingdoms

Lombard Italy

Lombard Italy began in confusion and violence. The bloody war between Byzantine and Ostrogothic armies left Italy exhausted and ripe for conquest. In 568, Alboin, a king who claimed (with what justification we will never know) descent from the royal family of the Gauti, led into Italy a motley army composed of provincial Romans from Pannonia, Suebians, Sarmatians, Herulians, Bulgars, and Gepids, as well as Saxons and Thuringians. Some were Arians, others orthodox Christians, and some probably still pagans. These groups had their own leaders, themselves members of royal or illustrious kindreds, jealous of one another and of the Lombard king. This was no federate army settling into a Roman province at the command of the emperor; it was a conquest, bloody and violent. The violence was exacerated by its decentralized nature, particularly after Alboin died at the instigation of his own wife, with individual dukes carving out autonomous duchies throughout Italy. They failed before the gates of Rome and Naples, and were thwarted by the *Roman* (we might as well say *Byzantine*) commander of Ravenna, while Burgundian and Frankish armies—following up on disastrous Lombard forays into Burgundy—captured the Piedmont valleys of Aosta and Susa and separated them from Lombard Italy.

Within their new duchies, the Lombards (who probably represented no more than 5–8 percent of the population in the territories they occupied) left no formal political role for those remnants of the Roman elite that had survived the Byzantine reconquest. A contemporary, writing in the western Alps, reported that Alboin's successor, Cleph "killed many of the higher and middling ranks."[1] Similarly, the eighth-century historian Paul the Deacon, relying on a near-contemporary history from the late sixth century, reported that "[Cleph] killed many powerful men of the Romans and others he drove out."[2] After Cleph's death, Paul continues that:

> In these days many of the noble Romans were killed out of greed. The rest were divided up among "guests" and made into tributaries, so that they should pay a third part of their harvests to the Lombards.[3]

Taken together, these passages seem to indicate that, during the conquest, many Roman landowners were killed or driven into exile, presumably into those regions still controlled by the Empire. Their lands were probably confiscated and retained as royal or ducal lands, if not redistributed among the Lombards. The other landowners were forced to pay a heavy tax of one-third of their yields to their conquerors, presumably the dukes and the king.

Such measures clearly subordinated the remaining Roman elite to their Lombard conquerors. Nevertheless, while heavily burdened with taxes, they were not reduced to slavery or serfdom. A small military elite could hardly have desired to eliminate the entire upper stratum of Roman society, even if such a move might have been possible. It was far better to maintain the majority of them as taxpayers.

Life under the Lombards may have been hard on what remained of the Italian elite, but it was not much worse than for those who continued to live under the protection of the Byzantine governor who held on to important portions of coastal and central Italy between Ravenna and Rome. In fact, life under the Lombards may have been better than under the "Romans." Pope Gregory the Great, writing at the end of the sixth century, complains of landowners in Corsica trying to flee *to* the Lombards rather than from them and that elsewhere individuals of all classes seemed at times more inclined to live under Lombard dominance than under the relentless exactions of agents of the imperial fisc.[4] All in all, the Roman population that survived the sieges and raids of the early decades seems to have found a place in the Lombards' new order. In time (how much, we are not sure), the result was an amalgamation of Lombard and Roman society.

Sources on the Roman population of the Lombard kingdom in the seventh century are extremely scarce. However, archaeological and rare written sources hint at a fusion of the heterogeneous population in the kingdom. First, the various groups who participated in the invasions coalesced into a new, unified Lombard identity.

Then these "new" Lombards and their numerically superior Roman neighbors merged into one.

Law was, initially, a major means of creating a Lombard people. From the mid–seventh century on, the heterogenous barbarian warriors serving in the kingdom were expected to follow Lombard law unless permitted an alternative legal tradition by the king.[5] Certainly, Lombard legal identity was not a matter of birth but of royal decree. Under royal pressure toward unity, references to the spectrum of groups comprising the army of Alboin disappear in favor of a simplified Lombard identity alongside that of Romans. But this dichotomy, too, began to fade. Gradually, the Lombards adopted Roman dress, began to use Roman pottery and other products, and, although our evidence is indirect, to intermarry at all levels. The clearest evidence of the Lombards' adoption of Roman tradition was their use of cities. The various duchies established across the kingdom (perhaps as many as thirty-five according to Paul the Deacon) all selected Roman towns as their centers.[6]

By the 700s, when written sources begin to reappear in Italy, the amalgamation of Lombards and Romans was greatly advanced. Families gave their children both Roman and Lombard names. Some even mixed name elements in the Germanic tradition, to produce hybrid names such as Daviprand or Paulipert.[7] Roman and Lombard legal traditions likewise became intertwined. Lombard law, written on the command of various kings between the 650s and the 750s, existed parallel to Roman law, and showed some influence of Roman practice, including, most fundamentally, the concept of a written code itself. Land law remained thoroughly Roman and, while inheritance law followed separate traditions, choices were being made about when to apply one or another of the codes.

By the early eighth century, Lombard law was available to all. A chapter of King Liutprand's law makes this explicit:

> In the case of scribes we decree that those who prepare charters should write them either according to the law of the Lombards— which is well known to be open to all—or according to that of the Romans; they shall not do otherwise than is contained in these laws and they shall not write contrary to the law of the Lombards or of the Romans."[8]

The edict goes on to say that, by mutual consent, people could go outside both laws and make a private pact between themselves. However, regarding questions of inheritance, documents had to be prepared according to the law. Some have interpreted this last phrase to mean that "Only when dealing with matters concerning inheritance did everybody have to stick closely to his or her law."[9] However, this may be an overinterpretation. The text simply says that, in cases involving inheritance, scribes had to write "according to law," that is, one or the other of the laws available to them. Presumably, a private deal would be inappropriate under those circumstances since it would affect third parties, that is, potential heirs, who had not consented to the private agreement. The law does not state that testators did not have a choice in which law to follow. Law had become a resource, not a fact of birth.

The written charters by which individuals transferred land show individuals choosing one law or another, with the choice differing even within families. Two examples analyzed by Brigitte Pohl-Resl are telling. In a charter of 767, a group of people made a donation to the Abbess of S. Salvatore in Brescia. No legal distinction was made in the charter concerning the legal position of the donors, and the fact that they shared in the property being donated suggests that they were kin. Nevertheless, one, and only one, who incidentally carried the Latin name of Benenatus (meaning "well-born"), indicated after his signature that he was to receive a return gift or *launegild* "according to his Lombard law."[10] Apparently Benenatus, alone of his kindred, had taken the option of claiming

Lombard law offered to all by King Liutprand. Again, in 758, a woman with the good Lombard name of Gunderada but explicitly designated as a Roman woman (*Romana mulier*), donated or sold a piece of property with the consent of her husband. This consent was normal and proper for a woman living under Lombard law. Under Roman law, it should have been superfluous. Whatever the designation of "Roman woman" might have meant, she and her husband were acting in accordance with Lombard legal tradition. Apparently, either Gunderada no longer followed Roman law or her Romanness meant little in a legal context.[11] These examples strongly suggest that, by the eighth century, the use of one or another law said little about anything that one could call "ethnic" identity of Italian landholders.

The relatively easy amalgam of Romans and Lombards may have been facilitated by the heterogeneous nature of the invaders, their decentralized rule, and their correspondingly mixed religious identities. In the mid–sixth century, a delegation to the Emperor Justinian had portrayed the Lombards as orthodox. By the time they invaded Italy, the Lombard army included orthodox Christians, pagans, and Arians.[12] Alboin seems to have been Arian, or at least a pagan sympathetic to Arianism, although his first wife— Chlotsuinda, daughter of the Frankish king Chlothar—was an orthodox Christian. Later kings might be Arian or orthodox, and a considerable portion of the Lombard population continued to practice paganism well into the late sixth century. With the exception of King Authari (584–590) who attempted to prevent Lombards from receiving orthodox baptism, Lombard rulers made no serious attempt to impose a uniform religion on their people. Local dukes were in a position to support or oppose religious practice, or to ignore it altogether. By the end of the seventh century, Lombard rulers and, presumably, the population at large, finally were absorbed into the orthodox faith of the majority of Italy's population without great drama or conflict.

The amalgamation of Romans and Lombards did not mean the loss of Lombard identity, however. Quite the opposite: Regardless of biological origins, or whether one's ancestors had actually arrived in Italy with Alboin, by the eighth century the social elite identified itself as Lombard. Only Lombards had access to power and wealth, but this meant not so much that Romans remained subordinate to the Lombards but rather that Romans had become Lombards. The meanings of both terms shifted in complex ways.

Lombard identity drew on the tradition of the military elite that had been the original group to enter the kingdom, regardless of the contemporary reality. To be a Lombard was, at least in theory, to be a free warrior and a property owner. This is the image presented in the *Lombard Laws* of the eighth century. The soldier (*exercitalis* in Latin, *arimannus* in Latinized Lombard) is the archetypical free man in the laws of King Luitprand (712–744).[13] By the time of his successor King Aistulf (749–756) the identity is subtly reversed. To be a man of wealth is to be a warrior:

> The man who has seven manses let him have his coat of mail and other military equipment, and let him have horses and the other armament. Likewise those men who do not have manses but have forty *iugera* of land should have a horse, a shield, and a lance. . . .

> Likewise, concerning those men who are merchants and who have money wealth: those who are the greater and more powerful let them have a coat of mail and horses, a shield, and a lance; those who follow them should have horses, a shield and a lance, and those who are lesser, let them have a quiver with arrows and a bow.[14]

In other words, if a person were sufficiently wealthy, he was then required to equip himself as a proper Lombard, regardless of his family tree.

And what of "Romans"? There are still Romans in Aistulf's code, but the code equates *Romanus* not with one who descends from the indigenous population of Italy or even one who follows Roman law, but as an inhabitant of that territory of Italy controlled by imperial authority, either directly through Ravenna or by the pope. The law forbids merchants to trade with "a Roman" without royal permission, under penalty of severe punishment, including having his head shaved and going about shouting, "In this way will those suffer who conduct business with the Romans without royal permission when we are at war with them."[15] Clearly the sort of "Roman" envisioned here is not an inhabitant of the Lombard kingdom—such wealthy merchants and traders were now by definition all Lombards—but a "foreigner" from Italian territory still under the control of Constantinople. Similarly, eighth-century court cases speak of "the time of the Romans" as that distant past before the Lombard kings came to rule Italy.[16] A new Lombard ethnogenesis had occurred, in which all landowning elites of the kingdom could participate, while *Romanus* had become an attributed political and territorial designation, closely identified with the power of the Byzantine state.

Visigothic Spain

The Gothic kingdom created in Gaul in 418–419 followed the model of late Roman federated accommodation that we saw in the previous chapter. For the first fifty years of Gothic rule, Gothic kings operated within this tradition of Roman federates. The Goths, whose numbers have been variously estimated between 80,000 and 200,000 men, women, and children, never comprised more than a tiny minority of the population of their kingdom. They were settled primarily in Gaul around their capital of Toulouse and had little presence other than some military units south of the Pyrenees. The vastly more numerous Romans continued to live according to Roman law and institutions, secure in their law and in their traditions. The end of this tradition came only in 466 when King Euric abrogated the treaty with the Empire and undertook a real conquest of southern Gaul and Provence to the east and of Spain to the south. Such a shift in policy resulted as much from the decayed political situation in Gaul and Italy as from any new Gothic ideological program. By the 460s, imperial military and political authority in the west no longer existed, and Euric was simply reacting to fill a vacuum of power.

The new expansionist Gothic program evoked a fierce reaction from elements of the indigenous population, especially in the Auvergne and south of the Pyrenees, in the Tarraconensis and throughout the Ebro Valley. The conflict was not strictly between Romans and Goths: In some areas, the Goths placed former Roman commanders in positions of authority. Still, local landowning aristocrats led the resistance, using barbarian federates of their own as well as their own retainers. The fighting was particularly brutal in the Ebro, where local interests were threatened not only by the end of the Roman-Gothic pact, but by increasing numbers of Gothic settlers who began to move into Spain for the first time in the 490s.

Nevertheless, even in this period of maximum friction between the Goths and their subjugated population, cooperation between Goths and Romans began in earnest. King Alaric II (484–507) took the lead in seeking an accommodation with his Roman subjects.

Alaric addressed two burning issues among the Gallo-Romans in his kingdom. The first was the need for a legal structure within which Roman subjects of the Gothic king could conduct legal matters among themselves. Relations between Goths and Romans were probably dealt with in the code issued by Alaric's father Euric, which applied to all inhabitants of the Gothic kingdom.[17] What was to be the law that governed transactions within the Roman community? Alaric settled this by issuing an updated and abbreviated version of the *Theodosian Code*, the basic Roman legal code since its promulgation in 438. The summary, known as the *Breviary of Alaric,* provided a royally sanctioned code for his Roman subjects, appropriate for the more basic realities of life in the Visigothic kingdom.

The second issue was the difficulty created by the fact that boundaries of Church dioceses, established before the disappearance of imperial rule, no longer corresponded to the geographical divisions of southern Gaul beween Franks, Burgundians, and Goths. In 506, although himself an Arian, Alaric summoned a Church Council in Agde to reassure the orthodox hierarchy and to settle the problems caused by the new political realities of the early sixth century.

Through these actions, Alaric managed to win the loyalty of the Gallo-Roman landowners in his kingdom. Even orthodox bishops showed themselves loyal to him, and by 507 an important contingent of Romans, under the command of the son of one of the most ardent anti-Gothic leaders of the previous generation, fought beside the Gothic king against the Frank Clovis at Vouillé.

But Alaric lost the battle and his life at Vouillé, and with him died both the Gothic kingdom of Toulouse and the possibility of a rapid rapproachment between Goths and Romans. As the survivors of the debacle and their families and retainers crossed the Pyrenees into central Spain, the reconstituted Gothic kingdom took on a more desperate and antagonistic cast. The Spain into which the retreating Gothic army moved its kingdom was a culturally diverse Roman administrative district. It included, along with a majority of Hispano-Romans, considerable populations of Greeks, Syrians, Africans, and Jews. These lived, for the most part, in port towns such as Tarragona, Tortosa, Elche, Cartagena, and in Narbonne, capital of the narrow strip of coast between the Pyrenees and the Rhone still held by the Goths after 507. In addition, the Suebi continued to rule Galicia, and there were native communities, including Basques in the north and others in Orospeda and

Cantabria, little touched by centuries of nominal Roman occupation. In these rugged and economically isolated areas, *Romanitas* had meant little more than intermittent military presence, and paganism continued to be fairly common well into the seventh century. Where Roman traditions were strongest, such as the Ebro Valley, the Visigoths had also encountered the strongest opposition in the previous generation. The defeated Gothic army that pulled back across the Pyrenees in 507 faced a monumental task if it were to bring unity to the Iberian peninsula.

The establishment of the Visigothic kingdom in central Spain might be seen as the final end of Gothic migration. In the sixth century, the Goths set about consolidating their position in Spain even as they maintained the *modus vivendi* with the Roman landowning elite established previously by Euric and Alaric. At the same time, they tried to maintain their separate identity through prohibitions against intermarriage and by the preservation of their Arian faith.

Among the elements of the *Theodosian Code* that had been adapted and included in the *Breviary of Alaric* was the prohibition against intermarriage between Romans and barbarians. In the *Theodosian Code,* the primary concern had been the very real problem of conspiracy between Roman provincials and their barbarian kinsmen.[18] The even stronger wording of the prohibition in the *Breviary,* which forbade Romans to marry "barbarians," may not even have meant to include Goths among the *barbari:* The real intent might have been to thwart Frankish-Roman marriage alliances deemed detrimental to Visigothic interests.[19] It may have been intended to protect Gothic identity, threatened after two generations of residence in a vastly more numerous population. But it may also have been intended to protect Roman rights, since an obvious means of acquiring Roman estates was a more or less coerced marriage of a Roman heiress with a powerful Goth. Whatever the original reason, once the Visigothic kingdom had retreated into Spain, the prohibition took on a new meaning in a new context. Now it was understood as a bar between Gothic and Roman marriages. In the aftermath of Vouillé, it characterized a concerted attempt to keep the Gothic military elite separate from the Roman populace. This prohibition remained in effect for fifty years. The desire to maintain a separate identity was shared by the religious leadership of the Hispano-Romans, who forbade orthodox Catholics to marry Arians.

For Arianism constituted the second element of Gothic identity. Through the sixth century, Goths clung to their religious tradition, and, through this same period, it divided them from the orthodox Roman population and offered fertile ground for Byzantine or east-Roman intrigue. Nevertheless, Gothic leadership considered such cultural borders essential, and even introduced new ones. In the early sixth century, for example, archaeological material hints that Goths may have self-consciously begun to dress themselves or at least their dead in a way that would mark themselves as distinct from their Roman neighbors.[20]

How effective these attempts to preserve a separate Gothic identity were is impossible to determine. Certainly some inter-marriages did take place between Romans and Goths, and certainly some conversions crossed the religious barrier. More significantly, while Romans enjoyed their property rights, they remained outside the realm of political power, and this probably encouraged some ambitious attempts to change identity. As one historian has pointed out, while these measures sought to preserve the distinctiveness of Goths and Romans, "Gothic laws do not however define what constituted a Goth."[21] In all likelihood, Gothic kings could decide whom they would consider Goths, and some motion across these barriers was not only possible but even necessary for the Gothic military to retain control of a far-flung kingdom. Certainly, as long at the Goths remained a small, separate, military elite, their ability to control all of Spain was greatly limited. By the middle of the century, the monarchy was plagued with assassinations, rivalries, and breakaway provinces. Rebels even invited the Emperor Justinian to intervene; as a result, the Byzantines occupied the southeast coast and threatened the kind of bloody reconquest that had destroyed Ostrogothic Italy.

By the 570s and 580s, however, all of the traditional means of separating Goths and Romans began to break down. The vigorous King Leovigild (569–586) strengthened and expanded royal authority throughout Spain. He put down revolts in Cordova and Orense, brought distant provinces, such as Cantabria and Asturia, under royal control, and even pacified, to some extent, the Basques. He established a permanent capital in Toledo; this at a time when kings of other barbarian kingdoms still practiced a peripatetic kingship without a fixed center of government. In 584–585 he defeated the Suebian kingdom of Galicia and incorporated it into his kingdom. As part of his program of centralization, he began to break down the traditional barriers separating his subjects. He repealed the prohibition against intermarriage, now understood unambiguously as a prohibition against Roman-Gothic union. His real purpose in so doing must have been to encourage Catholics to marry Arians, since Catholic Church legislation forbade intermarriage. Thus such unions, permitted by the crown but not by the Church, could be meaningful only if the Catholic partner were ready to ignore Church law. Leovigild further attempted to encourage Catholic conversions to the Gothic form of Christianity by holding a synod at Toledo that modified Arian doctrine insofar as it accepted the parity of the Father and Son (but not the Spirit) and removed the requirement that converts had to undergo a second baptism. Clearly Leovigild was trying to make it as easy as possible for Romans to become Goths.[22]

Leovigild's efforts at eliminating the barriers between Romans and Goths failed because of the strong resistance of the orthodox bishops. His own son, Hermenigild, saw a more effective means of consolidation. During a revolt against his father, Hermenigild converted to Catholicism, presumably hoping to garner support from the Catholic majority. Although Hermenigild's revolt was unsuccessful and ended in his exile and eventual death, his brother Reccared followed the same path after his father's death. He converted to Catholicism in 587 and led the rapid conversion of the remaining Arian bishops and the whole Church at the Council of Toledo in 589. At last, the majority of the population could begin a rapid assimilation. The goal was, in Reccared's own terms, no less than the creation of a new, unitary society—the "society of the followers of Christ, that transcended the traditional Gothic-Roman dichotomy."[23]

The conversion of the Goths left no barriers to social and cultural assimilation. If the Gothic language was still being used anywhere outside of Arian liturgy (highly unlikely by the seventh century), it quickly disappeared. Dress and material culture of Goths and Romans, long virtually indistinguishable, had become entirely one.[24] The last vestiges of distinct legal traditions for Goths and Romans disappeared in 643–644 when King Chindasvinth promulgated a code that applied to all the inhabitants of the kingdom.[25]

Although distinctions between Goths and Romans vanished, Gothic identity did not. However, just as the label *Lombard* in Italy had become a designation of class and wealth, in Spain to be praised for Gothic ancestry meant little more than to be of illustrious birth. What mattered was wealth, power, and identity with the kingdom, not ancestry. Kings, according to a canon of the Sixth Council of Toledo in 638 had to be "of the Gothic *gens* and worthy in character." But this simply meant that Franks or Aquitanians were excluded from the kingship.[26] King Erwig, who succeeded to the throne in 680, was the son of an exiled Roman from the Byzantine Empire. Hardly a Goth in any ethnic sense, he was nevertheless a Goth because he had been born in the Visigothic kingdom and could claim noble parentage from his father, who had married a relative of King Chindasvinth. Thus he satisfied the stipulations of the council. To be a "Goth" was to be a member of the Visigothic kingdom's elite.

The Catholic hierarchy threw themselves into support of this new vision—and of the Gothic kings who voiced it—with extraordinary vigor. The program of unifying society under Catholicism was directed, through the seventh century, by councils of Toledo, sixteen of which were held between 589 and 702. However, while conversion may have facilitated the unification of Goths and Romans, it did not take into account the reality that the "Roman" population of the peninsula had never been unified in culture or religion. The decades of Visigothic Arian control had worked to simplify the heterogeneous composition of both Goths and Romans. In the first stage, the various Arian Suebi, Vandals, Alans, and others had merged into a single *Populus Gothorum,* while the orthodox Greeks, Syrians, and North Africans in Spain had been forced into a single *Populus Romanorum.* When the Gothic king abandoned Arianism, these two "peoples" could become one. However, the process excluded a major part of the Roman population of Spain: the Jews.

Through the course of the sixth century, Jews progressively lost their Roman identity, as orthodox Christianity and *Romanitas* became ever more closely linked. They were thus forced into an ethnogenesis of their own, one that created them as a despised and persecuted people in the eyes of their Catholic neighbors. The increasing marginalization of Jews, in a society that saw a unified Christian identity as a defining characteristic, paralleled developments in the Byzantine Empire. There, too, as orthodox Christianity became an issue of state concern, Jews found themselves increasingly marginalized and persecuted. In the Visigothic kingdom, this marginalization and persecution was even more drastic than in Constantinople.

After the conversion of the Goths, as the distinctions between Roman and Goth disappeared, the otherness of Jews grew more evident and disturbing to the Christian kings. Visigothic Spain thus developed the most precocious and terrifying laws aimed at forcing the Jewish population of the kingdom into the *societas fidelium*.

Terrible pressures were brought to bear on Jews, who were faced with baptism or brutal punishment. Jewish travel was restricted and placed under the supervision of Christian clergy; adherence to Jewish dietary laws, circumcision, and proselytizing were punishable by flogging, scalping, mutilation, and confiscation of property. But even while these efforts were intended to bring about conversion, royal legislation implied that even converted Jews remained enemies of Christianity. Ultimately, anti-Jewish legislation reached the point that King Ervig ordered the enslavement of all Jews, whether converted or not.[27]

The vehemence with which the kings, supported by the clergy—including among them Julian of Toledo, himself of Jewish origins—sought to eliminate Jews was in sharp contrast to their actual ability to carry out the draconian measures that they ordered. The population at large apparently did not share this vitriolic hatred, and time and again the very shrillness of the legislation showed the lack of support for its measures. Nevertheless, the determination of the rulers to eradicate this "new" people that their policies had created left a terrible legacy in Spain, where, in the early modern period, these fanatical concerns about purity of blood re-emerged.

Frankish Identity to the Eighth Century

North of the Loire in the sixth and seventh centuries occurred a similar process by which a majority population came to adopt the identity of a ruling minority. In this world, far from the cultural and political centers of Empire, the process moved more rapidly and more thoroughly than elsewhere. Whether a calculated measure to win Gallo-Roman support in opposition to the Visigoths, an equally calculated affront to Ostrogothic hegemony, or a personal decision of a warrior-king seeking the most effective divinity, Clovis's conversion certainly facilitated a rapid amalgamation of Franks and Romans. Likewise, Clovis's sons and grandsons expanded their hegemony east without problems of ethnic or religious tension.

The assimilation of Romans and Franks did not mean the disappearance of overlapping notions of identity in the kingdom. The same regional identities that drew on local pride in *civitates,* apparent in the fifth century, continued in the Frankish world. The Frankish *coup d'état* did nothing to diminish this regionalism, although membership in the *Regnum Francorum* added a new layer to possible identities and loyalties. Clovis and his successors absorbed the administrative divisions of the Roman *civitates* and established their capitals in the old Roman administrative centers. Thus, these same *civitates* remained the focus of regional pride and identity, just as they had been in Late Antiquity, with local elites, now including both descendants of regional aristocracies and agents of the Frankish king identifying themselves with their city. Merovingian military organization re-enforced these identities, since military musters saw units organized under the command of their local counts. This military organization also prolonged other late Roman forms of identity, particularly that of barbarian military units stationed across Gaul. These small settlements retained their military command and thus a specific identity through the seventh century. One hears thus of Saxons in Bayeux, Taifali in Poitou, Chamavari in Langres, Scoti in Besançon, and Suebi in Courtrai.[28]

The kingdom of Clovis was not the kingdom of the Franks. It was but one of several Frankish kingdoms, and as he and his descendants absorbed both their Frankish rivals and the kingdoms of their neighbors to the east and south, they came to terms with regional identities, even as they placed their own supporters in key positions of power. Ultimately, three Frankish kingdoms emerged in the course of the sixth century: Neustria, the western region centered on Soissons, Paris, Tours, and Rouen, in which the Franks had first emerged to defend and then replace imperial rule; Austrasia, the regions east of the Rhine but also Champagne, Reims, and, later, Metz; and Burgundy, a kingdom including the old kingdom of the Burgundians along the Rhone and much of Gaul, reaching to the capital of Orléans.

The region between the Loire and the Rhine remained the center of Frankish power. Here, regardless of ancestry or military affiliations, the elite population rapidly came to identify itself as Frankish. By the middle of the sixth century, even descendants of the family of Bishop Remigius of Reims, the Roman bishop who had baptized Clovis, carried Frankish names and no doubt considered themselves, and were considered, Franks. Neustrian and Austrasian elites alike considered themselves one people, and even their most violent struggles were seen as civil wars rather than wars against aliens. Certainly the population was governed by a territorial law, the so-called *Salic Law*, only portions of which were written down for the first time in the early sixth century.[29] Originally intended for the followers of Clovis, the written versions of the law were amended and expanded by a progression of Frankish rulers over the next century. By the second half of the seventh century, the *Salic Law* was generally assumed to be the law of those living in the western Frankish kingdom, Neustria.

Eventually, in Austrasia, another version of royal edicts and custom coalesced into the *Ripuarian Code*. The final version of the *Lex Ribuaria* is a Carolingian text, revised by Charlemagne, and some argue that the entire code dates from no earlier than the later eighth century.[30] However, the text shows influence of the *Burgundian Code* and the *Salic Law*, and assumes that there is an unwritten Ripuarian law outside of the written *Code* itself. All this sug-

137

gests that some sort of law code for the Austrasian kingdom was created, probably in the early seventh century, as part of the growing regionalization of the Frankish world.

Beyond the boundaries of the Loire and the Rhine, Frankish political and military organization created new regional identities, building, in part, on local aristocracies and their Roman or barbarian traditions, but transforming them into new social and political entities. In regions such as Burgundy and Aquitaine, older traditions of law and social structure were adapted to the new Frankish system. Elsewhere, Franks imposed rulers and law codes.

The Frankish conquest of the Burgundian kingdom turned the region into a Frankish subkingdom without eliminating the preexisting aristocracy or their legal traditions. This region on the upper Rhone had been ruled by a mixed barbarian army settled in the Jura region by the Roman commander Aetius around 443 that had expanded into the regions of Vienne and Lyon in the last decades of the fifth century. In 517 the Burgundian king Sigismund had issued a law code, the *Liber Constitutionum,* which combined earlier royal edicts, some Burgundian customs, and Roman vulgar law.[31] A central concern of the code was to regulate relations between the barbarian and Roman inhabitants of the kingdom, but it also modified and expanded on Roman law in matters strictly among Romans. In so doing, the code effectively grouped the non-Roman population into a single "people," and was itself both evidence and agent of a stage in the continuing ethnogenesis of the Burgundians.[32] By the time of its compilation, the *populus noster* ("our people") addressed by Sigismund were the inhabitants of the kingdom, whether Roman or barbarians.

The Frankish conquerors incorporated the Burgundian kingdom into a larger kingdom consisting of much of the territory around Orléans. At the same time, they respected the Burgundian social and legal tradition, leaving it intact through the sixth, seventh, and eighth centuries. Even a dispute between the Merovingian chamberlain and a forester, when tried in the old Burgundian capital of Chalon-sur-Saône, was conducted according to the Burgundian law of trial by combat.[33] Throughout the seventh and eighth centuries, the area's aristocracy jealously guarded a sense of regional Burgundian identity, preserved in its unique legal tradition.

Such regionalization was even more pronounced in the conquered areas east of the Rhine, in Alamannia, Thuringia, and Bavaria. The Merovingians governed these areas through dukes, regional commanders of Frankish origin, installed by the force of Frankish arms but maintained through ties of kinship and patronage with the local aristocracies. These duchies were not composed simply of pre-existing peoples from the Migration Period: Rather, they were Frankish creations, molding, dividing, and reconstituting regional elements into new territorial principalities.

South of the Loire, in the regions of Aquitaine and Provence captured by the Franks, regional identities based on continuity with local aristocratic families absorbed Frankish governors who tended to "go native." The result was that regional strongmen created powerful regional alliances that, while professing loyalty to distant Frankish kings, managed their own affairs. Here Roman law, in the *Theodosian Code* or in abbreviated forms such as the *Breviary of Alaric,* provided the uniform territorial law for all, and counts and dukes (or, in Provence, patricians) developed powerful regional identities. Similar processes took place in areas east of the Rhine, such as Alamannia, Thuringia, and especially Bavaria, where Frankish agents merged quickly with local aristocracies. Tensions certainly existed, and, when central Frankish authority was preoccupied with their own problems, powerful separatist movements could create virtually autonomous principalities. However, these movements were aristocratic and involved alliances of rebellious Frankish officers and their local allies. They were hardly prompted by nationalist or ethnic sentiments.

The creation of powerful regional identities—each with its own law and its own aristocracy, but each orthodox and tied to central Frankish authority—led to a fundamental change in the uses of ethnic terminology, as it had been used for centuries. Through the fourth and fifth centuries, the fundamental divisions of society had been between Romans and barbarians, a dichotomous world equally accepted by both sides, as well as by those whose very lives showed how little such simplistic divisions corresponded to reality. Although in Classical Antiquity *barbarian* was a term of at least mild opprobrium, in the military world of Late Antiquity, federated armies were content to accept the term as a neutral or even positive designation of their non-Roman identity, a collective identity much more stable than the myriad "tribal" names that might be attached to their individual families and armies. By the beginning of the seventh century, such a distinction meant nothing. Roman citizenship was meaningless; regional populations were divided by social stratum, not by language, custom, or law; and all of society, again with the exception of the Jewish minority, were united in a single faith. Thus the term *barbarus* began to take on a new meaning: that of foreigner, and increasingly, pagan foreigner.

In the life of Colombanus, written in the first quarter of the seventh century, *barbari* can be the pagan Alamanni or the Arian Lombards, but never the Franks or the Burgundians.[34] When Christians are called *barbari*, as in the eighth-century book of miracles of St. Austregisil, which so designates the Frankish army of Pippin I, this is clearly meant as a negative commentary on a violent enemy, an enemy that, even if Christian, behaved like stereotypical pagans.

With the disappearance of barbarians from the Empire, Romans vanished as well. One could argue that this took place even more rapidly. The sixth-century historian Gregory of Tours, often seen as representative of the Gallo-Roman aristocracy, never uses the term to designate himself, his family, or those whom he considered his social and cultural equals. Instead, he uses the regional etiquettes in favor since the third century, or he speaks of the senatorial class. There are no Romans in Gregory's history.[35] Other Frankish sources use the designation more freely, particularly in the formulaic descriptions of the family origins with which saints' lives often begin.[36] By the eighth century, the term had become a regional designation, largely confined to Aquitanians in the west and to Raetians in the Alps. Finally, around the middle of the ninth century, *Romanus* is used in the Frankish realm exactly the way it was used in the Lombard kingdom: to designate persons from the city of Rome. Within the western Roman Empire, there were no more Romans or barbarians.

The New Barbarian World

The power vacuum left by the integration of the Lombards and other peoples into the Empire during the fifth and sixth centuries was quickly filled by new and different societies: east and north of the Rhine by the Saxons, along the lower Danube by the Avars and by the Slavs. These "new" barbarians re-established the bipolarity that had vanished within the confines of the Empire, but did so in a very different and long-lasting manner.

Of these new peoples, the Saxons were most like their predecessors, the Franks and the Alamanni. Since the third century, Saxon pirates from the North Sea coast had raided the Empire, and units of Saxons had served in the Roman army for almost as long. One band of Saxons in the fifth century appeared in Gaul, commanded by Odovacer, presumably the same barbarian king who later made himself ruler of Italy.[37] Like the Franks and the Alamanni, they were not an "ancient" people but, rather, decentralized bands, operating independently. Their name, commonly believed to be derived from a short, one-edged sword or sax, gives no clue to a cohesive self-identification. They were by no means the

141

only warriors to use this weapon, which may have been Hunnic in origin and not Saxon at all.[38]

In Britain, some of the Saxon federates, recruited by locals to defend the island after the departure of Roman troops in the early fifth century, made themselves masters of the eastern portions of the Roman province. Gradually, joined by other opportunistic Saxons, Angles, Jutes, Franks, and Frisians from the mainland, these warrior bands, coalesced into small principalities, warring with, and occasionally allying with, equally unstable principalities of Romano-Britains. Originally pagan, these Saxons became Christian in the course of the seventh century. They were converted, in part, through the efforts of Roman missionaries, in part by Irish monks, and in part by the quiet work of the indigenous Christian population who, like the Romans of Lombard Italy, Spain, and Gaul, merged with these conquerors to form a new society.[39]

The Saxons on the Continent maintained their decentralized organization and their pagan identity. Through the sixth and seventh centuries they seem to have had a relationship to the Frankish world remarkably parallel to that of the Franks and the Roman Empire two centuries previously. The Franks thought of the Saxons as a dependent people, obligated to pay tribute in the form of cattle or to provide defense against the even more distant Wends. At times, Merovingian kings launched punitive expeditions against them reminiscent of those led by Emperor Julian against the Franks and the Alamanni. At other times Saxons joined Frankish military campaigns, as when they entered a coalition against the Frankish Duke Charles Martel in the early eighth century.[40] The Saxons probably saw themselves and their relationship to the Franks quite differently. Into the late eighth-century reign of the Frankish King Charlemagne, they maintained their fierce independence, their religion, and their own traditions.

If the Saxons had taken the place of the Franks and the Alamanni to the West, the Avars assumed the roles of the Goths and

Huns to the East. This steppe confederation, fleeing the Turkic expansion in Central Asia, appeared in the Carpathian basin in 567 and in 558–559 sent an emissary to the Emperor Justinian, offering to fight against the Empire's enemies in return for annual payments.[41] In many fundamental ways they resembled other steppe peoples who appeared in Europe in the first millennium.[42] These nomads developed a highly specialized form of survival, based on pastoralism, that allowed them to live in regions otherwise unsuitable for human settlement. Traveling hundreds of miles in seasonal migrations necessitated the development of complex forms of organization and communication. These ecological imperatives developed into characteristic forms of political and social organization. Mobility, flexibility, and mounted warfare were essential for survival. So, too, was the need to combine with other, similar groups and thus develop enormous steppe empires over a rapid period of time. We have already seen this in the short-lived Empire of Attila's Huns. Where the Avars differed from their predecessors, however, was in their ability to transform themselves from just another steppe people into a fairly centralized and institutionalized, polyethnic kingdom between Byzantium and the western kingdoms that survived, in victory and defeat, for 2½ centuries.

The Avars achieved this feat because they managed to establish hegemony over the disparate peoples along the Balkan frontier of the Empire and to monopolize the name *Avar* to an extraordinary degree. For some twenty years, Baian, the ruler or khagan of the Avars, fought Utigurs, Antes, Gepids, and Slavs until he had created a large, polyethnic confederation. Following the departure of the Lombards, Baian firmly established his rule in Pannonia. In 582 he captured the old Illyrian capital of Sirmium. His sons felt strong enough to challenge Constantinople itself: In 626, a vast army, composed of Avar horseman and Slavic ships, began an attack on the city coordinated with Persian allies. The siege lasted

143

little more than a week and ended in an Avar defeat. Such a catastrophe might easily have meant the end of Avar hegemony. Indeed, some of the subject groups attempted to go their own way following the disaster, but the core held, although it was greatly diminished. A century later, Avar horsemen raided west into Bavaria and Italy until they finally met their superior in the person of Charlemagne. Charlemagne penetrated into the center of the Avar kingdom in modern Hungary, and destroyed the Avars' ability to maintain their polyethnic confederation. Within a generation and without a major battle, the Avars vanished from history.

If the Avar confederation disappeared without leaving more than rich graves across eastern Austria and Hungary, it nevertheless played a fundamental role in the creation of the most important and enduring phenomenon of Eastern Europe: the rapid and thorough Slavicization of Central and Eastern Europe.

Between the fifth and the seventh centuries, eastern portions of the area long considered Germania, as well as the Balkan and Black Sea provinces of the Empire from the Baltic to the Mediterranean, came to be controlled by Slavs. This transformation took place without great fanfare, without tales of powerful kings like Attila, Theodoric, or Clovis; without heroic migrations or desperate battles. It was a process that left no written evidence from the Slavs themselves, and its internal dynamic was even less noted and understood by Byzantine and Latin observers than were the Germanic ethnogenesis processes of Western Europe. And yet the effects of Slavicization were far more profound.

In the west, barbarian federated troops absorbed Roman systems of government, religion, and settlement. They ultimately became thoroughly Roman, even while changing utterly what this term meant. The Slavic migrations did not adopt or build on Roman systems of taxation, agriculture, social organization, or politics. Their organization was not based on Roman models, and their leaders were not normally dependent on Roman gold for

144

their success. Thus, their effect was far more thorough than anything that the Goths, the Franks, or the Saxons ever achieved. Almost everything about the early Slavs—their origins, their social and political structures, and their tremendous success—has been an enduring puzzle.

Scholars have long debated the "original home" of the Slavs. The question of origin is probably as meaningless to ask for the Slavs as for other barbarian peoples, formed as they were through amalgams of what Roman sources termed Scythian or Sarmatian and Germanic populations in the regions east of the Elbe, left behind by the military elites who formed the Germanic armies moving toward the Empire. Recent scholarship has argued convincingly that the "birth" of the Slavs took place along the Byzantine frontier under the influence of Byzantine military and economic pressure, much as that of the Franks and the Alamanni along the Rhine had centuries before in the west.[43] However, Slavic culture was much closer to the soil and more deeply attached to agriculture than the fast-moving Frankish and Alamannic armies that became Roman federates and, eventually, conquerors. With their light plows, small-scale agriculture, and small, individually organized social units, Slavs did not simply arrive as tax-collecting armies but as farmers who worked the lands they conquered.

For conquer they did. Their spread was slow but violent, followed by the absorption of indigenous populations into their linguistic and social structures. But this expansion was uncoordinated and radically decentralized. Into the high Middle Ages, Slavic language and material culture presented a remarkable unity across Eastern Europe, but this was in radical juxtaposition to an equally radical lack of indigenous political centralization. The sixth-century Byzantine historian Procopius described how they were "not ruled by one man, but they have lived from old under a democracy, and consequently everything which involves their welfare, whether for good or for ill, is referred to the people."[44] This decentralization was perhaps the key to their success: Without kings or large-scale chieftains to bribe into cooperation or to defeat and force into service, the Byzantine Empire had little hope of either destroying or co-opting them into the imperial system.

Gradually, across the seventh century, Slavic warrior-settlers moved across the Danube and into the Balkans. The chronology is unclear and necessarily so: The process was so decentralized and fluid that it could hardly be dated or documented. Individual reversals at the hands of Byzantine counteroffensives could not stop such a widespread process. Nor did conquest simply mean transfer of tax revenues, as it had for the victims of Germanic conquest two centuries before: Slavs either killed the soldiers they captured or sold them for ransom. Those who remained faced flight or absorption into the Slavic peasantry. In this society of soldier-farmers, there were no other options.

When large-scale, hierarchical organization of Slavic groups did take place, it was almost inevitably done according to leadership structures introduced from outside. These might be Germanic or Central Asian leaders, whose model of ethnogenesis provided the possibility of greater concentration of power and greater subordination of individuals and groups. Fundamental to this process were the Avars.

The Slavicization of a wide band from the Elbe to the lower Danube was already well underway before the arrival of the Avars. The Avar settlement may have increased the Slavic pressure against the Byzantine frontier, as Slavic bands fled this new steppe Empire. This may explain the early Slavic invasions of the Greek peninsula in the latter half of the sixth century, soon to be followed by Slavic armies under Avar command. Others were absorbed into it and became a permanent fixture within the Avar kingdom. The Avars demanded winter quarters from their Slavs, requisitioning horses, supplies, and women from them, as needed. In times of war, they used tributary Slavs as infantry and, during the siege of Constantinople, as a navy. However, they seem to have also been prepared to treat some of their Slavic communities with more restraint, offering gifts to their headmen in return for troops and support. Byzantine chroniclers described the Slavs as the oppressed subjects of the Avars; Western observers described the Avars and Slavs as allies rather than as rulers and ruled. Both were probably correct.

Avar political and military structures provided the context for the ethnogenesis of specific Slavic groups. In the early seventh century, probably in the aftermath of the debacle before the walls of Constantinople in 626, considerable portions of the Avar periphery revolted, carving out autonomous polities between the Avar kaganate—to the west, the Franks; to the east, Byzantium.

In the region that is now probably the Czech Republic, a Frank, Samo, organized a band of mixed-parentage Slavs who had rebelled against the Avars into a formidable union. According to a Western source, the Slavs elected Samo king, and he ruled a Slavic kingdom for over thirty-five years.[45] The hiving off of Samo's Slavs from the Avar confederation following the Avar failure to capture Constantinople in 626 was probably only one of several such revolts against the defeated Avar Kagan.

The various groups known in the tenth century as Croats and Serbs probably had their origins in this same period of internal crisis in the kaganate. The early history of the Croats is impossible to disentangle entirely and is based almost entirely on the account of the Byzantine emperor Constantine Prophyrogenitus (905–959).[46] Constantine wrote a treatise for his successors on how to administer the Empire that paid particular attention to the Empire's Slavic neighbors. He drew both on contemporary experience and on now-lost materials in imperial archives going back centuries, but it is impossible to know exactly how dated, or indeed how accurate anything that he says really is. Constantine speaks of two groups of Croatians, those he calls the "White" Croats living near the Franks and the Croats in Dalmatia. He provides a mythical genealogy according to which once upon a time the Croats lived "beyond Bavaria" but a family of five brothers and two sisters split off from them, led their people to Dalmatia, where they defeated the Avars and then further divided into different groups. Actually, the Croatian name appears in various areas on the periphery of the former Avar kaganate, in what is modern Germany, the Czech Republic, Austria, Moravia, Slovenia, and Greece, as well as in modern Croatia. Attempts to establish proof of some ethnic unity for all these groups, perhaps predating the arrival of the Avars, has proven impossible.

Certainly, the term *Croat* does not appear in any source from before the middle of the ninth century as the designation of a people or tribe. The term *Croat* probably originally designated either a social stratum or was the title of a regional office within the kaganate.[47] Such an explanation would explain why this term, which is not a Slavic word, might eventually designate a Slavic "people" without having to imagine that there had once upon a time been a non-Slavic Croatian people. It also accounts for the appearance of "Croats" on opposite ends of the kaganate without having to imagine great migrations or a family of brothers, each of whom establishes a different part of a Croatian people. Probably, in the course of the eighth and ninth centuries, these breakaway groups, identified as "Croat" by their leadership or organization in the Avar kingdom, gradually coalesced into separate polities with invented ethnic identity and a fanciful genealogy.

Just as Constantine posits a people known as the "White" Croats related to the Croats of Dalmatia, he tells of Serbian origins in a people known as "White" Serbs living beyond the land of the Huns, bordering the Frankish kingdom and White Croatia.[48] Again he reports a genealogical legend: Two brothers take half the people and request protection from Emperor Heraclius. The emperor then settles these Serbs in the province of Thessaloniki. Later, they decide to return to their homeland, and when they ask permission of Heraclius's commander at Beograd, they are given land in what is now Serbia. This legend, like that of the Croats, places the origins of the Serbs in the period of the Avar debacle before Constantinople, explains the presence of Serbs on distant ends of the Avar kingdom, and accounts for the emergence of a new "people" who carry another non-Slavic name in the Balkans. Rather than mining the legend for historical evidence on the origins of the Serbs, it should probably be seen as part of the rapid centrifugal forces tearing at the Avar kaganate following its defeat.

A similar origin can be seen for the Bulgars. Romans had encountered peoples of this name since the fifth century around the Black Sea. They, along with other -*gur*-named groups, such as the Kutrigurs, the Onogurs, and the Ogurs belonged, in Roman eyes, to the Huns, that is, to Central Asian steppe warriors. In the aftermath of 626, however, rebels against the Kagan are regularly called Bulgars. Again, as in the case of the Croats, the diversity of the Bulgars is explained later in the legend of five brothers, the sons of the Onogur Kuvrat who revolted in the 630s, threw off Avar control, and united the Bulgars around the Black Sea. At the same time, Bulgar refugees from an unsuccessful revolt in the western regions of the kingdom fled to Bavaria, where they were first welcomed by the Frankish King Dagobert and then, after being dispersed for the winter, set upon, and killed by royal orders.[49] In the following generation, a Bulgar leader, Kuver, revolted against the Avars and led a mixed population of descendants of Roman prisoners who had been settled in the Avar kingdom fifty years previously south to Thessaloniki.[50] Possibly in the seventh century the names Kuvrat, Kuver, and Croat may all have originated in a title and only come in time to designate individuals or peoples. In any case, none of these groups—be it Samo's kingdom, the Croats, or the Bulgars of Kuver—were pre-existing peoples revolting against Avar lordship. Rather, they were peoples in the making, forming in opposition to the Avars, but organized in some way according to institutions or principles taken from their lords.

Over the course of the following centuries these groups, whose non-Slavic names may be derived from Avar titles, developed from political units, created in opposition to their Avar masters, into "peoples," complete with genealogically informed origin myths that explained their origins in ethnic terms rather than in terms of political organization.

By the early eighth century, then, political rather than ethnic identities characterized populations in what had once been the Roman Empire. For those people who mattered enough to be described in the scarce written sources of the period, their identification with a geographically defined kingdom determined how they were designated and, to a great extent, how they described themselves. Of course, this terminology was derived from earlier centuries, although the social realities that it designated had become quite different. Franks were the elites of the Frankish kingdom; Lombards were their counterparts in northern Italy, as were Goths in Spain until the conquest of the Iberian peninsula by Berber and Arab armies in 711. The free inhabitants of the English kingdoms were Saxons. Romans were the inhabitants of those areas of Italy under papal or Byzantine control, or else they were the inhabitants of Gaul south of the Loire. Regional identities, of course, still counted for much, as they always had. The Frankish rulers controlled Thuringians, Bavarians, Frisians, and Alamans, although these were provincial designations, not tribal ones.

Beyond these stable polities, the world more resembled that of the fifth century. Saxons, a collective term for decentralized pagan Germanic peoples, inhabited the northern borders of the Frankish world, while in the East, a vast, polyethnic Avar Empire spanned Byzantium and the West, spawning "new" peoples such as Croats, Serbs, and Bulgars. These groups—Saxons, Avars, and their progeny—were the new barbarians, the only barbarians left in Europe, just as the only Romans were the inhabitants of Rome.

Chapter Six

Toward New European Peoples

By the early eighth century, even as some of the ancient names of peoples first encountered in Late Antiquity continued to be used, their content and meaning had changed radically. Relatively stable kingdoms had appeared across Europe, kingdoms that drew their labels from the old "gentile" names, but that included all of their Christian inhabitants within the community so designated. Even contemporaries did not distinguish clearly between ethnic, political, and territorial terminology: The *regnum Francorum* was not exactly the area of Francia. A monk could translate *Germania* as *Franchonoland*.[1] At the same time the terms *Francia* and *Gallia* could be used interchangeably. Within this region, the small military settlements of Saxons, Alans, and others across Gaul that had maintained some sort of military identity since the fifth and sixth centuries, were all but gone. Peoples had become once more what they were for Pliny: territorial units of geographical and political organization, not social or cultural groups.

The rapid conquest of Spain by Berbers and Arabs in 711–712 changed this picture south of the Pyrenees. On the one hand, religion became an important new distinguishing element in Iberian identity, as it had not been since the conversion of the Visigoths to orthodoxy. On the other, even though the Muslim conquerors made no concerted effort to convert the Christian and Jewish populations, elites began to convert to Islam shortly after the conquest and, by the tenth century, Spain was a majority Muslim society.

Elsewhere, by the 720s, the western half of the old Roman world had developed into autonomous petty kingdoms ruled by petty princes or by regional strongmen who often took the title of duke, a title that emphasized independent military command. On the continent, in Neustria, the old heartland of the Franks, ducal families maintained their puppet kings of the Merovingian dynasty. But in Austrasia, the eastern Frankish realm, an upstart ducal family dominated the political arena and claimed control of the West as well. The other regions of the Frankish kingdom had gone their own way: In Aquitaine and Bavaria, autonomous dukes toyed with claiming royal authority; in Brittany, Frisia, Saxony, Thuringia, Alamannia, Burgundy, and Provence, dukes or dukelike patricians ruled, at times in the name of the Merovingians; at times in proud disdain of them. These units were not unlike the autonomous Lombard duchies that characterized central and southern Italy or the petty kingdoms that made up the political frameworks of Anglo-Saxon England and Wales. Everywhere local political elites dominated small-scale polities. Their positions may have been hotly disputed within the local power structure but competition was based on internecine aristocratic rivalry, not on cultural or ethnic differentiation. Regionalism seemed triumphant.

Later in the eighth century, the expansion of the Frankish Empire east, north, and south to include much of the low countries, western and central Germany, the Lombard kingdom, and Catalonia might have been expected to continue the convergence of ethnic, political, and geographical identity. Instead, the wars of expansion fought by the Frankish kingdom under its Carolingian kings introduced a new role for ethnic and legal differentiation within Europe as one of the building blocks of the Empire.

It took over a generation for the upstart Austrasian ducal family of Pippin II and his son Charles Martel to crush their Neustrian opponents and to consolidate their control in the old Frankish heartland. They then began to crush and absorb the peripheral duchies around them. This they accomplished through ruthless military campaigns, but also by co-opting factions among the local notables, to whom they promised a share in power and their own dominant position guaranteed by their local law. Thus, east of the Rhine, as duchies were brought under Frankish control, they were at the same time granted their own laws that protected their subordinate but distinct identities. These codes drew, in part, on local tradition and recognized regional practice but they relied primarily on Frankish authority.

Most of these codifications took place in the eighth century under Carolingian command. However, they claim a greater ancestry, pointing back to the early seventh century, the apogee of Merovingian royal power under Clothar II (584–623) and Dagobert I (623–639). Thus, while guaranteeing that local communities could preserve a judicial identity, this very identity was being forged even as it was projected backwards onto a distant, mythic past in order to confer legitimacy on it by infusing it with an ancient aura. The preface to the Bavarian code, for example, claims that the code had been drawn up around the start of the seventh century, in the days of King Dagobert the Great. There may indeed have been a Bavarian legal tradition since the seventh century, but the code that proclaims this ancient past is an eighth-century creation. Similar archaizing prefaces in other codes, while perhaps echoing some element of previous legislation, largely mask the recent origins of these legal compilations.[2]

West of the Rhine, in Burgundy, Provence, Septimania, and Aquitaine, the Carolingians took a similar tack. Here local elites

153

who cooperated with the new powers were able to preserve their autonomy by retaining Roman, Burgundian, or Gothic law under the wider umbrella of Frankish lordship. Such guarantees were particularly important in areas that bordered Islamic Spain and Lombardy, since local collaboration was essential for Frankish stability.

But Frankish legal policy had another edge to it: Even as it guaranteed legal traditions to recently absorbed regions of the Empire, this policy allowed royal agents, wherever they were, to retain their legal autonomy as well. Thus, royal officials and soldiers could settle in these distant areas without having to live according to local legal custom. Like European agents of Empire in the nineteenth century, they enjoyed extraterritorial status wherever they went. This "personality principle" underwent a major expansion when the Franks conquered the Lombard kingdom in 773–774. Soon Frankish, Burgundian, and Alamannic "colonists" were establishing themselves in the conquered kingdom, proudly preserving their particular legal status and transmitting it to their children. This patchwork of legal systems, requiring every individual who appeared in court to declare his or her law, long outlived the Carolingian political system. Into the eleventh century, families proudly claimed distinctive legal status long after their ties with the regions from which their ancestors had migrated had disappeared.

The Carolingian regional policy of co-opting local elites—by guaranteeing them a public place and a separate law while planting imperial agents throughout a vast Empire—created a new kind of European ethnicity. This identity was grounded more in legal privilege than in ancestry or culture. It did not define people in their entirety but only in terms of certain rights.

This restricted form of legal identity, developed in the context of Carolingian imperial expansion, long survived the Carolingian Empire. It became the model employed in the colonization of the Slavic world in the twelfth and thirteenth centuries, when "Saxon" peasants were granted not only land but the right to live according to their law as islands in recently "pacified" eastern areas. In time, the right to claim Saxon or German law because a right to special privilege, which could be granted to anyone, regardless of ancestry.[3]

However, at the same time that Carolingian imperial policy was creating new meanings for old labels, Carolingian ideology was inventing ancient genealogies for them. Just as the new codifications of regional laws emphasized their antiquity, Carolingian historiography showed a marked interest in the early history of these new social and legal entities, particularly the Franks themselves, but also Lombards and others, projecting them into a distant past. Thus, the Carolingian imperial system created its own justification through genealogies of peoples, its own "imagined communities," while claiming for the Frankish people a universality and divine mission that superseded that of Rome. The success of this invention has survived the Frankish Empire itself by more than a millennium: From the age of the Crusades into the twentieth century, *Frank* was a term used by Greeks and Muslims for Western Europeans.

Concluding Reflections

What we see in summary, then, is the long term, discontinuous use of certain labels that have come to be seen as "ethnic." Classical ethnographers, even while deeply aware of the heterogeneous nature of their own societies, readily projected these quasi-organic biological images onto the "other," the "barbarian." One can wonder whether the communities and polities living on the fringes of the Roman world would have recognized themselves in the stereotypes generated by Roman observers. However, from the fourth century on, military bands appropriated these labels and used them as rallying cries for concerted action. The names of peoples were thus less descriptions than claims—claims for unity under leaders who hoped to monopolize and to embody the traditions associated with these names. At the same time, these leaders were appropriating disparate traditions and inventing new ones in the form of the royal and sacred genealogies, legendary battles, and heroic events of these peoples.

The success of some of these military groups in institutionalizing themselves in the provinces of the Roman Empire brought about enormous changes in how these terms were used and in the social realities they proclaimed. With victory and territorialization, bold claims created the reality that they asserted and, in a matter of generations, social and political groups with widely differing pasts, values, and cultures accepted the victor's right to articulate for them a common past. Myths of common descent and a shared history, myths molded less by indigenous oral tradition than by classical ideas of peoplehood, masked the radical discontinuity and heterogeneity that characterized Late Antiquity.

Territorialization and conquest in the eighth and ninth centuries co-opted regional elites and benefited imperial agents, whose status and privileges were protected by new forms of personal law and masked in an antiquarian interest in possible ancient pasts that could provide an ideology of distinction.

What does all this have to say about the contemporary re-emergence of ethnic nationalism with which we began this book? The short answer would be "Nothing." The flux and complexities of Late Antiquity belong to a different world from the simplistic visions of ideologues. But such a response is too simple. When contemporary nationalists appeal to history, their notion of history is static: They look to the moment of primary acquisition, when "their people," first arriving in the ruins of the Roman Empire, established their sacred territory and their national identity. This is the very antithesis of history. The history of European peoples in Late Antiquity and the early Middle Ages is not the story of a primordial moment but of a continuous process. It is the story of political appropriation and manipulation of inherited names and representations of pasts to create a present and a future. It is a history of constant change, of radical discontinuities, and of political and cultural zigzags, masked by the repeated re-appropriation of old words to define new realities. The Franks "born with the baptism of Clovis" are not the Franks of Charlemagne or those of the French people Jean Le Pen hoped to rally around his political movement. The Serbs who came into existence in the decaying remains of the Avar Empire were not the people defeated at the battle of Kosovo in 1389, and neither were they the Serbs called to national aggrandizement by Slobodan Milosevic. The Albanian victims of Milosovic's Serbs were not the Illyrians of the sixth century Balkans. Nor is this process at an end: The peoples of Europe are a work in progress and always must be.

At the same time, the history of Europe's peoples is itself part of the problem of European ethnicity. We historians are necessarily to blame for the creation of enduring myths about peoples, myths that are both tenacious and dangerous. By constructing a continuous, linear story of the peoples of Europe, we validate the attempts of military commanders and political leaders to claim that they did indeed incorporate ancient traditions of peoples. By accepting the myths created by authors of Late Antiquity and the Middle Ages as historical, we too often propagate and perpetuate such claims. At the end of our survey of European origins, let us attempt to step outside of our Western focus for a moment and consider the history of another people on another continent. Let's compare European peoples and one of the great peoples of Africa, the Zulu.

Europeans As Zulu

A fundamental obstacle to any attempt to revise the popular understandings of European peoples is that these perceptions have penetrated so deeply into European consciousness that they no longer are understood as historical reconstructions but rather as self-evident and essential components of national identity. They lie outside the domain of history, in that realm of collective memory that is all the more powerful for being mythic. Perhaps the best way to escape the centuries of assumptions and confusions that have accumulated concerning the identity of European peoples is to try, at least for a moment, to escape from Europe. To that end, we will examine the birth of a different people in a distant region, the Zulu of southern Africa. However, it is easier to move one's geographical perspective than one's analytic categories, as we shall see.

Attempting to understand early Zulu history poses the same problems, for many of the same reasons, as does an attempt to understand the early history of European peoples. The resemblances between Zulu and Franks, Goths, or Serbs operate at two levels: First, the first texts that attempt to record the history of their migrations were written under influences similar to those of Judeo-Christian and classical traditions. Thus, the "classic" story of Zulu ethnogenesis includes the same mythical, literary, and classical motifs that we find in European history. The reason for this similarity is that the people who first attempted to write a history of the Zulu were European missionaries, steeped in both biblical and classical concepts of ethnogenesis. In this they resemble nothing so much as the "narrators of barbarian history" who told similar stories, from similar perspectives, in the sixth, seventh, and eighth centuries.[4]

Second, even when the assumptions and projections of the author of Zulu "national history" are removed, the very different image of Zulu ethnogenesis that emerges bears different but no less remarkable similarities to more modern and scientific analyses of European ethnogenesis. These similarities suggest that, beyond the myths of genesis narratives within and outside of Europe, certain similar social and political forces may have been at work in the creation of these very different societies. They may also suggest that constructs and analogies, distorting though they may be, are an inevitable part of historical comprehension.

Some Europeans may bristle at seeing the origins of their own ethnic and political groups equated to those of a southern African people. For many, the reason may be less specifically racism than the deeply held belief that while the "history" of an African people may be a mere cultural construct, their own past is somehow "real." I would invite readers to suspend their cultural chauvinism for a moment and entertain the possibility that they are no different from the millions of South Africans who trace their origins to Shaka KaSenzangakhona, the founder of the Zulu nation, who shares the same place in his people's history as does Clovis for the French, Chrobatos for the Croats, and Isperihk for the Bulgarians.

The Zulu are one of the largest and most self-conscious peoples of southern Africa. Through the Inkatha Freedom Party, at once a Zulu cultural movement and a political party, the influence of the roughly 5 million Zulu extends far beyond the apartheid KwaZulu homeland, established in 1971 and which today forms the province of KwaZulu-Natal. Zulu identity is closely tied to its historical memory, a memory that stretches back to 1830, when the Zulu kingdom was the most powerful independent African state in the southern portion of the continent, and beyond the early nineteenth century to its distant origins in the seventeenth and eighteenth centuries. This memory should seem strangely familiar to Europeans.

The father of Zulu history, however, was no Zulu. He was, rather, A. T. Bryant (1865–1953), a Christian missionary who, decades after the death of Shaka KaSenzangakhona, first recorded a continuous account of Zulu history. According to Bryant, this history begins in the sixteenth century, when the Nguni peoples, including the ancestors of the Zulu, migrated into the region of southeast Africa from the north and northwest, possibly, according to some Zulu, from as far north as the modern Sudan. As the Nguni moved south, they dispersed into a number of "clans," the essen-

159

tial political and social units of society. These clans were all descended from a common ancestor and were ruled by that ancestor's direct living representative. By the early sixteenth century, the Nguni were settled around the upper Vaal River, where they divided into two parts. The group first moved away to the northwest and was eventually absorbed into the Sotho migrants moving down from the north. The other, purer Nguni clans, the Ntungwa, the Mbo, and the Lala—all sharing a common origin and culture—moved south into the Phongolo-Mzimkhulu region, which they settled at roughly the same time. The Ntungwa settled into what is today the Zulu heartland, where they established their numerous clans under largely independent chiefdoms. Around 1670, one clan leader, Malandela, or at least his family, crossed the Mpembeni and Mkumbane streams, over the Mtonjanei heights, and then into the Mfule Valley. Here, a few generations later, was born Zulu, a descendant of Malandela and the eponymous founder of the Zulu clan.

Sometime in the eighteenth century, several chiefdoms abruptly began to centralize their political power and expand their territorial control over neighboring clans. This rapid change has been explained as the result of pressure from ecological change or demographic growth that outstripped the food supply. It was made possible by the emergence of particularly gifted and ambitious leaders, the most prominent of these being Shaka KaSenzangakhona, leader of the Zulu, who, together with Dingiswayo, leader of the Mthethwa, subjugated almost all the neighboring clans and drew their young men into the Zulu army. The one exception were the Ndwandwe, a highly centralized and militarized expansionist society, similar to the Zulu. Around 1817, the Ndwandwe defeated the Mthethwa and killed Dingiswayo.

Soon after the death of Dingiswayo, Shaka defeated the Ndwandwe and, in a rapid series of conquests, established Zulu rule over a wide area of southeast Africa. Even Shaka's murder in

1828—at the hands of two of his half-brothers, allegedly because of the growing discontent with his despotic rule—did not destroy the Zulu state that he had created. The Zulu kingdom, although gradually weakened by conflicts with other nations and especially with the Boers and the British, maintained its cohesion and strong sense of ethnic identity even beyond its final defeat by the British at the end of the nineteenth century. Still today, Zulu ethnic identity—fostered by this common memory of its past independence and unity, and symbolized by the *inkatha* or woven grass coil—remains a powerful motivating force in southern Africa.

This memory is indeed powerful, but it is also imaginary. The "history" of the Zulu ethnogenesis is a modern creation, constructed from internal views of how the world ought to be and from external schemas of how a people's history ought to read.

A. T. Bryant, the collector of Zulu "history," brought to his work essential assumptions about the nature of his sources, his subject, and the broader framework of intelligibility, which fundamentally transformed the Zulu into a "people." The manner in which he approached the oral traditions he collected rests on two linked assumptions.[5] The first is a naive approach to the oral traditions themselves, which he assumed were to be taken as historical fact, fragmentary and confused perhaps, but qualitatively the same as the overarching narrative Bryant was constructing. He assumed that there had to be a single "correct" version of the Zulu past, but that different individuals might have reported a more or less distorted version of the historical truth. Thus, the historian's task was to fill in the gaps, link disconnected bits of information, and harmonize discrepancies. The role of the historian was, he declared, "the simple one of bringing together, in one place and in some systematic order, all such information concerning the *Earlier Tribal History of the Natives of Zululand and Natal*."[6]

His second assumption was that these oral traditions were the histories of ethnically united "Nguni" clans, which endured, with

161

little change, for hundreds of years and which had their own political, social, and residential boundaries. His history of the rise of the Zulu kingdom, then, was a straightforward account of the amalgamation of these discrete entities into the Zulu clan. Thus, he assumed that the past was essentially the same for hundreds of years, and clan structures of the nineteenth century could be projected backwards onto the earliest Nguni period.

Bryant not only accepted without question the historical accuracy of the legends he collected, but he organized these according to his own intellectual and cultural preconceptions, preconceptions that he assumed were part of the natural order. Bryant was a Christian missionary, writing, he states, out of a sense of altruistic duty "to our unlettered Negro brother to rescue for him from final oblivion, before too late, such of his simple traditions as are still recoverable, whatever be their worthlessness to us."[7] He arrived in southern Africa in 1883, some fifty years after the death of Shaka. Thus he had no firsthand knowledge of the history he reported, gathering instead what he could from the king's nephews and their generation. He combined this information, which he described as "fragmentary, disconnected, and oftentimes quite meaningless to the uninitiated,"[8] into a single picture in a manner he compared to that of an artist assembling a mosaic[9] for a European reading public. Bryant had a low opinion of the European public, which he characterized as one "to which all history is proverbially insipid," and for which, therefore, he necessarily had to present the material in a manner such that "the reading might be made endurable, and the interest be sustained."[10]

The results of Bryant's background, sources, and public are obvious in the mosaic he formed from his fragments. First, as a Christian with a classical education, he organized his material to make explicit parallels between the Zulu and both the Hebrew people's wanderings in *Exodus* and the legendary wanderings of the Lombards, the Goths, and the Slavs in the early Middle Ages. Bryant compares the relationship among divisions of the Bantu, of which the Nguni are a part, to "that existing in Europe between the English, Germans and Scandinavians of the Nordic race."[11] Malandela is explicitly compared with Moses, the melons his family found on their journey the "manna in their wilderness."[12] Like Moses, Malandela "was fated but to see the Promised Land and die."[13] Thus Bryant consciously understands the Zulu history in terms of biblical models and, more generally, in terms of European history. If the story of the Zulu migration resembles a story familiar to European readers, that is so, in part, because it is intended to be.

Second, not only did Bryant structure the Zulu history into a Hebrew or European ethnogenesis, as he understood it, but the manner in which he assigned motivation and meaning likewise mirrored European traditions. This, too, was intentional. Again, because he assumed that his European audience would find his material both "unattractive" and "alien to its understanding," he announced his intention to

> make our historical reading intelligible and pleasant—by assuming, in general, a light and colloquial style; by creating here and there an appropriate "atmosphere"; by supplying it a necessary "background"; by inducing a proper frame of mind by an appeal to pathos; by clothing the "dry bones" of history in a humorous smile; by uniting disconnected details by patter of our own based on our knowledge of Native life and character.[14]

Much of this effort to make the alien more familiar to European readers consisted of drawing constant parallels to European cultural traditions. Dingiswayo, for example, became "the chivalrous knight" and Bryant compared his Empire building favorably to that of leaders of ancient Egypt, Persia, Greece, and Rome:

Only modern England has succeeded in rising to this height of imperial statecraft, and has been universally voted wonderfully wise in
consequence. The Negro, however, who did precisely the same
thing, and long before, has never been regarded as more than "a
mere benighted savage."[15]

Shaka, by contrast, was, in Bryant's view, the Zulu Julius Caesar;
he titles the chapter in which he recounts Shaka's murder "Caesar
Falls, and Tyranny Is Dead." The result is that, both in his narrative of migration and centralization and in the cultural sense he
makes of his evidence, Bryant did not record and preserve a Zulu
internal voice. Rather, he created it by molding fragments of Zulu
traditions into "real history," that is, a meaningful narrative that
draws its meaning from history par excellence—that of the Judeo-
Christian-Roman world.

Bryant was hardly the first ethnographer to describe the origins
of a "people" in terms derived from biblical and classical proto-
types and to structure his account according to the cultural assumptions and prejudices of his audience. This is exactly what authors at the end of Antiquity and in the early Middle Ages did when
they wrote accounts of the origins of the Goths, the Lombards, the
Franks, the Anglo-Saxons, and, later, of the Serbs, the Croats, and
the Hungarians. As we have seen repeatedly in previous chapters,
authors such as Jordanes, the historian of the Goths; Gregory of
Tours, writing about the Franks; or Constantine Porphyrogenitus,
describing the Slavs, while claiming explicitly or implicitly to convey ancient oral traditions, were casting their peoples in Romano-
Christian categories. Names of leaders, the divisions of peoples
into tribal or familial units, epochal battles and legendary wanderings, all carried great symbolic value and were frequently linked
to the history of the Hebrew *Exodus* narrative and traditions of
Greco-Roman ethnography. Such histories were never really "national" histories, intended to convey the indigenous understand-

ing of a people's past. Rather, they were grounded in the author's political and cultural concerns and were restructured in order to advance the author's own contemporary agenda. Moreover, these authors, no less than Bryant, were hardly naive, indigenous witnesses, recording the traditions of their own peoples. Although some, like Jordanes and the Lombard historian Paul the Deacon, might claim descent from the people they described, they were thoroughly acculturated into the Roman Christian cultural tradition through which they perceived the material that they treated.[16]

Given Bryant's naive approach to his subject and sources and his explicit effort to re-create the Zulu past in a European mold, one might conclude that his efforts, far from making Zulu history accessible, make it unknowable instead. His account appears less like a mosaic than a hall of mirrors, each reflecting some aspect of his own cultural and political perspective without allowing any insight into Zulu ethnogenesis itself. Were one to take such a position, then one would conclude that *Olden Times in Zululand and Natal* tells us much about Christian missionaries in colonial Africa and nothing about Zulu history. Indeed, just this point has been argued about the historians of the early Middle Ages. But such a radical skepticism is unwarranted.

Bryant's mosaic may indeed be a fiction, but the individual fragments are not.[17] Alternative ways of understanding them and using them to construct an image of Zulu prehistory, particularly when combined with archaeology, permit historians to understand a very different Zulu past, in spite of Bryant's fanciful creation.

Recently, African historians have begun to sketch a "reconceptualized history" of the Phongolo-Mzimkhulu region by reinterpreting the oral traditions collected by Bryant, according to two fundamentally different criteria. First, they recognize that oral traditions are not simply factual accounts but, rather, "political" statements that impose on the past patterns of meaning that are intended to provide legitimization for programs of the present and future. Nor do these traditions reflect only a single ruler's values. Often they are the product of struggles among different factions and incorporate disjunctive and internally contradictory patterns in an attempt to neutralize the antagonism between competing factions. Historians can "unpack" these inconsistencies to rediscover something of the political conflicts that produced them, practicing a sort of textual archaeology, uncovering layers of claims and counterclaims, couched in the language of tradition, which official versions have attempted to obscure.[18]

Second, they recognize that the units of analysis, "tribes," "clans," and other political and social units, are not stable, objective, and enduring realities. Rather, the polities of the past and present change constantly in composition, internal organization, culture, traditions, ethnic affiliations, and boundaries.[19] Neither the Nguni nor the Zulu can be taken as objectively existing, stable actors in history. Rather, they are constructs, whose nature and very existence must be questioned constantly.

The history that emerges from a re-examination of the evidence based on these preliminary considerations is radically different from that created by Bryant and adapted as their own by contemporary Zulu. The homogeneous ethnic group Bryant called the Nguni never existed. *Nguni,* rather like *Germans,* has meaning only as a linguistic designation, never as a political, cultural, or social grouping. Likewise, the Ntungwa, the Mbo, and the Lala, which he saw as ancient divisions of the Nguni, were probably unrelated groups whose existence began in the process of the consolidation of the Zulu kingdom in the 1820s. Moreover, the migration Bryant described in biblical terms never took place. The archaeological record and a close reading of Zulu legends provide no evidence of long-distance population movements in the seventeenth and eighteenth centuries, anymore than one can accept the legends of Gothic migrations from Scandinavia or Frankish wanderings from the Danube to the Rhine. Rather, the groups that would, in time, become Zulu emerged from the indigenous population of the area. Migration stories are means of projecting mythic "founding charters" onto nineteenth-century polities.

Before the political transformations of the nineteenth century, the population of the region lived in numerous, small-scale units of various size and political structure. Some were small groups with chiefs who exercised ritual authority but little coercive control. Others were larger, with subordinate chiefs and a paramount chief who exercised considerable power over his subordinates. While political cohesion was supported by the redistribution of tribute paid to the chief by his supporters, other kinds of ties, including kinship, clientship, marriage, and neighborhood cut across these political boundaries. The result was that communities and chiefdoms were fluid, constantly growing, splitting, disappearing, and re-forming, through both peaceful and violent means, as elements of the mix realigned themselves according to the different variables.

The power of a chief was limited by the fluidity of these groupings, by the lack of institutions through which he could maintain prolonged command over the manpower of his group and prevent hiving off, and through the inability of a ruling group to acquire exclusive control over a chiefdom's basic economic resources, primarily land. These limitations also prevented the emergence of sharp class boundaries, based on access to economic resources. Even the authority of paramounts, or chiefs who commanded other chiefs, was limited by a chief's inability to legislate or coerce subordinate chiefs beyond the payment of tribute and the occasional mobilization of manpower. Again, lacking permanent central organs of control, paramountcies, too, were unstable, constantly dissolving into new forms.

The changes in the later eighteenth century that gave rise to powerful, centralized polities, such as the Mabhudu, the Mthethwa, and the Zulu, cannot be explained by the simple appearance of great military leaders like Dingiswayo and Shaka or simply by

167

such mechanical explanations as climatic change, ecological crisis, or spontaneous population growth. Rather, a major, external factor appears to have been the incorporation of the Phongolo-Mzimkhulu region into the European commercial system. This incorporation began with the penetration of European ivory traders into the area. Trade allowed chiefs who could control trade routes and supplies of ivory, and later of cattle, to expand their power through the distribution of European goods, especially cloth and metal. This change in relative power destroyed the traditional equilibrium within the system of growth, competition, disintegration, and transformation, which had characterized fluid social and political structures in the region.

The result of competition among chiefs for control of the benefits of international trade led to rapid transformation of the social and political organization of their chieftaincies. In particular, chiefs transformed *amabutho* or circumcision schools—groups of young men of roughly the same age who were periodically banded together under the ruling chief to undergo initiation rituals—into means of extending their power. These bands, with their own loyalties and identities, were put first to the task of hunting elephants on behalf of the chief for ivory, thereby increasing his wealth, his circle of clients, and his coercive power to obtain tribute. Since much of this largesse could be directed toward the *amabutho,* the process strengthened his control over these bodies of young men. In time, they became increasingly militarized, being used in conflicts with rival chiefs and in controlling subordinates and exacting tribute from recalcitrant subjects. As the dependence of the chiefs on their *amabutho* increased, so too did their need for cattle with which to reward them, a need that could be met only by raiding other chiefdoms and, in time, by territorial conquest to acquire prime grazing lands.

The specific means by which conquered neighboring groups were absorbed varied, from incorporation of existing chiefs into fictive origin traditions to isolation of the conquered as permanently subordinate to the ruling faction, creating a two-tiered form of social stratification.

By the early nineteenth century, this process of military expansion and political consolidation had created a number of large polities, with the conflict between the Ndwandwe, a highly centralized and militarized state, and the Mthethwa, a less centralized polity, led by Dingiswayo, in which subordinate chiefs, including Shaka of the Zulu, continued to enjoy considerable autonomy. Around 1817, the Ndwandwe defeated the Mthethwa and killed Dingiswayo, in part because Shaka had withheld Zulu support from his paramount chief. Shaka, his warriors intact, was able to use his forces to defeat the Ndwandwe and then rapidly expand control over the entire region.

The system of political control established by Shaka was an adaptation of that used by the preceding paramount chiefdoms. The youth of subjugated chiefdoms were forced into Zulu *amabutho,* required to live in segregated royal homesteads, and forbidden to marry without royal approval. This system weakened traditional ties uniting young men with older generations and bound them, both ritually and politically, to the Zulu king. Young women, too, were established in *amabutho,* through which the king could control the female labor force as well as marriages, which could be contracted only with designated members of specific male *amabutho* who had obtained permission to marry. In addition, high-status young women presented to the king as tribute were kept in secluded royal quarters as "daughters" and "sisters" of the king so that he could distribute them in marriage to powerful men as a source of royal patronage.

The result was a three-tiered Zulu society. The top tier comprised the king and the aristocracy, members of the Zulu ruling house, those incorporated into it early on in its expansion, and chiefs of subjugated chiefdoms. The second tier was composed of

169

the *amabutho,* the main prop of Zulu power. To cement them, they were encouraged to identify themselves as all of Ntungwa descent, thus sharing a common origin and past.

Just as members of the second tier were intentionally united by appeal to ethnic solidarity, members of the lowest tier—composed of conquered people on the margins of the kingdom, who were assigned menial roles and excluded from the *amabutho*—were portrayed as ethnically separate and inferior to the Ntungwa.

Shaka's conquests and consolidation took place with enormous violence. Groups fleeing his conquests moved far from Phongolo-Mzimkhulu, causing a ripple effect of instability in the region. His consolidation also met strong resistance from within, culminating in Shaka's assassination in 1828. However, the institutions he had created remained strong enough to survive his demise, and the kingship passed without serious incident to Dingane, his half-brother who participated in the assassination. Likewise, the creation of a myth of fictive descent in Zulu society was so effective that, by mid-century, Europeans were complaining that even the descendants of the chieftaincies conquered by Shaka saw themselves as the direct descendants of the Zulu who had conquered their grandfathers.

Zulu and Europeans

Both versions of Zulu history should be familiar to Europeans. Legends of a great migration, the gradual splintering of ethnically homogeneous clans, sudden rapid political change under demographic pressures, and the emergence of a powerful military state should sound familiar to anyone with even a passing knowledge of the Great Migration period of European history. It is the story not only of the Zulu, but of the Germanic and Slavic peoples as well. It takes no great imagination to see, in Malandela or Shaka, King Theoderic of the Ostrogoths, the Lombard leader Alboin, the

Frankish Clovis, the Croat Chrobatos, or the Bulgar Isperikh. On one level, this is because the ancient and medieval authors on whose word historians have relied for a history of these stood in almost exactly the same position vis-à-vis their subjects as did Bryant vis-à-vis Shaka. Gregory of Tours, Jordanes, Bede, and Paul the Deacon, for example, were all Christian authors, making implicit and explicit comparisons between the "peoples" about whom they wrote and the "peoples" par excellence, the Hebrews and Romans. Likewise, the very process of writing a history that included these peoples meant an attempt to incorporate them into "history"; that is, universal history, which for them could only mean the history of Rome.

Of course, Bryant was not simply mimicking authors of a thousand years ago. Very much a person of the late nineteenth and early twentieth centuries, he was, rather, modeling his history on the work of European historians who were equally under the spell of biblical and medieval models of social and cultural analysis. Part of the reason that his work received such widespread acceptance was that his image of the history of the Zulu seemed consonant with how Europeans and Europeanized Africans thought that societies were supposed to have come into being.

The revisionist interpretations of Zulu history by scholars such as Wright and Hamilton have reversed this tendency. They have begun to look behind the constructs of European ethnic mythology to understand the more complex and dynamic forces that brought the Zulu into being. Their work, which is less dependent on European models, offers an alternative model for understanding Zulu origins, and by implication, the formation of European peoples as well. One can see a convergence between how twenty-first European historians are revising their understanding of medieval ethnogenesis or people formation, and the ways that Africanists are approaching their subject. The effects of the Roman Empire, with its military and especially commercial links

171

in the barbarian world, are increasingly seen as a major destabilizing force, propelling changes in the barbarian world. New forms of military organization and the exercise of power by local chieftains, who could tap into Roman wealth and military support, made possible new and enormously powerful polities. Many of these were short-lived. Others managed to survive beyond the lives of their founders, to absorb other, rival groups, and to create a unifying myth of peoplehood, a myth that projected the people back into a distant, glorious past and justified claims for a great and powerful future.

If the similarities in the mythic histories of European peoples and the Zulu are similar, so too are the political uses of these histories. The Zulu past is a powerful tool in contemporary South Africa, claimed by all political factions in KwaZulu-Natal. In 1994, in a dramatic conflict played out, in part, before live television cameras, the Zulu nationalist prime minister and leader of Inkatha, Mangosuthu Buthelezi, attempted to prevent a rapprochement between the newly elected South African president and African National Congress leader Nelson Mandela and the Zulu king Goodwill Zwelithini by blocking the former's participation in the traditional celebration of Shaka Day. Buthelezi attempted to defend his nationalist position by appealing to the history of the Zulu kingdom since the times of Shaka. Such a bid to enlist history in the service of politics is reminiscent of European nationalists such as Slobodan Milosevic's manipulation of the anniversary of the battle of Kosovo or Jean Marie Le Pen's attempts to capitalize on the anniversary of the baptism of Clovis.

A few years ago, an American journalist traveling in the Greek province of Macedonia, after having been taken to numerous archaeological sites by his official guide to "prove" that Macedonia had always been and must remain Greek, commented on the importance of history for his host. The Greek replied, "You Americans don't understand. For us, history is *everything*." But a history that does not change, that reduces all the complexities of centuries of social, political, and cultural change, to a single, eternal moment, isn't history at all.

Those who claim that their actions are justified or compelled by history have no understanding of change, the very essence of human history. The history of the peoples of Europe in the early Middle Ages cannot be used as an argument for or against any of the political, territorial, and ideological movements of today, any more than the future of KwaZulu-Natal can lie with the "correct" interpretation of the life of King Shaka.

Of course, the past matters, and the complex, often violent and ever obscure process by which European peoples and nations have come to the present cannot be dismissed by catch phrases like "imagined communities" or "invented traditions." But, as we have seen, the image inherited from nineteenth-century history in the service of nationalism is no more appropriate. Within and outside the Roman world, social and political groups were always complex, ever-changing communities in which membership, goals, and identity were constantly open to negotiation, to dispute, and to transformation. From the start, the barbarian peoples across the Rhine and the Danube were never homogeneous language and cultural groups, bound together by ancestry or even by common tradition. Instead, they were every bit as complex as the Roman people itself. As the boundaries between Roman and Barbarian dissolved, what today is called "identity politics" became one means of organizing and motivating followers: New constellations claimed names of "ancient" peoples. Old polities vanished into the melting pot of Gothic, Hunnic, or Frankish lordship. Some were never to reappear. Heterogeneous groups of adventurers and defeated enemies agreed to accept a common leader and, in time, a common identity. In other circumstances, opposition leaders, claiming to embody the ancient tradition of a peo-

173

ple, might lead their followers to conquest and a new future or else to annihilation.

The one constant tendency was for successful groups to establish territorial kingdoms in which the politically significant elements of society increasingly accepted the identity of their leader. What peasants and slaves may have thought of themselves we will never know. But those inhabitants of kingdoms who fought together and who stood as free men in royal courts and assemblies recognized their commonality with their king. But such identity in autonomous kingdoms was one matter. As the Frankish Empire spread in the course of the eighth and ninth centuries, regional identities could be transformed into tools of Empire. Multiple identities, for different purposes and under different circumstances, were among the resources of Europe's elite.

Nor indeed did the process of change end with the emergence of recognizable medieval kingdoms. The history of the people of Europe has not ended—it never will. Ethnogenesis is a process of the present and the future as much as it is of the past. No efforts of romantics, politicians, or social scientists can preserve once and for all some essential soul of a people or a nation. Nor can any effort ensure that nations, ethnic groups, and communities of today will not vanish utterly in the future. The past may have set the parameters within which one can build the future, but it cannot determine what that future must be. Peoples of Europe, like peoples of Africa, America, or Asia, are processes formed and re-formed by history, not the atomic structures of history itself. Heraclitus was right: One cannot step into the same river twice. Those rivers that are peoples continue to flow, but the waters of the past are not those of the present or future. Europeans must recognize the difference between past and present if they are to build a future.

Notes

Introduction

1. *Le Monde,* September 24, 1991.

2. On the contested tradition of civic versus ethnic identity in the United States, see Gary Gerstle, *The American Crucible: Race and Nation in the Twentieth Century* (Princeton, 2001).

3. Charles F. Adams, ed., *Familiar Letters of John Adams and His Wife, Abigail Adams, during the Revolution* (New York, 1876), p. 211.

4. *Le Monde,* September 24, 1991.

5. *Der Standard,* June 23, 1992.

6. *Le Monde,* July 19, 1991.

Chapter One
A Poisoned Landscape

1. Benedict Anderson, *Imagined Communities: Reflections on the Origin and Spread of Nationalism* (London, 1983).

2. Miroslav Hroch, *Die Vorkämpfer der nationalen Bewegung bei den kleinen Völkern Europas: Eine vergleichende Analyse zur gesellschaftlichen Schichtung der patriotischen Gruppen.* Acta Universitatis Carolinae Philosophica et Historica Monographica XXIV (Prague, 1968).

3. See the summary in Ivo Banac, *The National Question in Yugoslavia: Origin, History, Politics* (Ithaca, NY, 1984), p. 28.

4. Ibid, p. 29.

5. Paul Freedman, *Images of the Medieval Peasant* (Stanford, 1999).

6. Mireille Schmidt-Chazan, "Les origines germaniques d'Hughes Capet dans l'historiographie française du Xe au XVIe siècle," in *Religion et culture autour de l'an mil: Royaume capétien et Lotharingie,* Dominique Iogna-Prat and Jean-Charles Picard, eds. (Paris, 1990), pp. 231–344, esp. p. 240.

7. For example, Martin Cromer, *De origine et rebus gestus polonorum* (1555).

8. Florin Curta, *The Making of the Slavs: History and Archaeology of the Lower Danube Region, ca. 500–700 AD* (Cambridge, 2001).

9. E. J. Hobsbawm, *Nations and Nationalism since 1780* (Cambridge, UK, 1990); see pp. 20–21 and note 19 for additional literature.

10. This brief summary draws largely on Otto W. Johnston, *The Myth of a Nation: Literature and Politics in Prussia Under Napoleon* (Columbia, SC, 1989) and Johnston, *Der deutsche Nationalmythos. Ursprung eines politischen Programms* (Stuttgart, 1990).

11. Johnston, *Myth of a Nation,* p. 25.

12. Johnston, *Myth of a Nation,* p. 10.

13. Johann Gottlieb Fichte, *Addresses to the German Nation,* R. F. Jones and G. H. Turnbull, trans. (Westport, CT, 1979). Reprint of the 1922 edition, published by Open Court Pub Co., London and Chicago, IV, pp. 52–53.

14. See Maurice Olender, *The Languages of Paradise: Race, Religion and Philology in the Nineteenth Century* (Cambridge, MA, 1992), esp. chap. 1, "Archives of Paradise," pp. 1–20.

15. E. B. de Condillac, *Essai sur l'origine des connaissances humaines* (1746), II, I, G. Le Roy, ed. (Paris, 1947), p. 103; cited by Olender, *The Languages of Paradise,* p. 5. See also H. Aarsleff, "The Tradition of Condillac: The Problem of the Origin of Language in the Eighteenth Century and the Debate in the Berlin Academy before Herder," in H. Aarsleff, *From Locke to Saussure: Essays on the Study of Language and Intellectual History* (London, 1982), pp. 146–209.

16. Fichte, *Addresses to the German Nation,* vii, 313–314.

17. See W. B. Lockwood, *Indo-European Philology* (London, 1969), p. 22.

18. In general, on the relationship between German philology and nationalism, see the essays in Benno von Wiese and Rudolf Henß, eds., *Nationalismus in Germanistik und Dichtung. Dokumentation des Germanistentages in München vom 17.–22. Oktober 1966* (Berlin, 1967), esp. Eberhard Lämmert, "Germanistik—Eine deutsche Wissenschaft," pp. 15–36.

19. Cited by R. Howard Bloch, "New Philology and Old French," *Speculum* 65 (1990): 40. See also his "'*Mieux vaut jamais que tard*': Romance, Philology, and Old French Letters," 36 *Representations* (1991): 64–86.

20. Bloch, "New Philology," p. 40.

21. Bloch, "New Philology," pp. 41–42: "*La* canso *des troubadours sont des plants indigene, nées spontanément sur le sol de la patrie.*"

22. On language and nationalism, see, among others, Hobsbawm, *Nations and Nationalism,* pp. 51–63, and Anderson, *Imagined Communities,* chap. 5 and passim.

23. See Bjørnar Olsen and Zbigniew Kobylinski, "Ethnicity in Anthropological and Archaeological Research: A Norwegian-Polish Perspective," *Archaeologia Polona* 29 (1991): 9–11.

24. Gustaf Kossinna, *Die Herkunft der Germanen* (Würzburg, 1911); *Ursprung und Verbreitung der Germanen in vor-und frühgeschichtlicher Zeit* (Würzburg, 1928).

25. Chris Wickham, *Early Medieval Italy: Central Power and Local Society 400–1000* (Totowa, NJ, 1981), p. 68.

26. Hobsbawm, *Nations and Nationalism,* pp. 48–49.

Chapter Two
Imagining Peoples in Antiquity

1. Herodotus, *The Histories,* II, 17.

2. Ibid., V, 48.

3. Ibid., I, 144.

4. Ibid., IV, 7–10.

5. Ibid., IV, 110–116.

6. Arnaldo Momigliano, *The Classical Foundations of Modern Historiography* (Berkeley, 1990), esp. pp. 5–10.

7. Herodotous, *The Histories,* I, 135.

8. Ibid., III, 38.

9. Edward W. Said, *Orientalism* (New York, 1978), p. 2.

10. Margaret T. Hodgen, *Early Anthropology in the Sixteenth and Seventeenth Centuries* (Philadelphia, 1964), p. 44.

11. Pliny, *Natural History,* IV.

12. Ammianus Marcellinus, *Histories,* XXII, 8, 42.

13. Ibid. XXIII, 6, 64.

14. Livy, *Ab urbe condita,* " . . . *nec sub eodem iure solum sed etiam nomine omnes essent, Latinos utramque gentem appellavit,*" I, 2.

15. Ibid., "*in populi unius corpus,*" I, 8.

16. Cornelius Tacitus, *Agricola,* XXX, " . . . *atque ubi solitudinem faciunt, pacem appellant.*"

17. Ibid., 33.

18. For a general discussion of Roman attitudes toward non-Romans see J. P. V. D. Balsdon, *Romans and Aliens* (Chapel Hill, NC, 1979).

19. Jeremy DuQuesnay Adams, *The* Populus *of Augustine and Jerome: A Study in the Patristic Sense of Community* (New Haven, 1971), p. 110.

20. Augustine, *De Genesi contra Manichii*, I, 23. See also Adams, *The* Populus *of Augustine and Jerome*, pp. 48–49.

21. Augustine, *City of God*, XIX, 24. "*Populus est coetus multitudinis rationalis rerum quas diligit concordi communione sociatus.*" See also Adams, *The* Populus *of Augustine and Jerome*, p. 19.

22. Ammianus Marcellinus, XVI, 12, 26. On the Alamanni, see Dieter Geuenich, *Geschichte der Alemannen* (Stuttgart, 1997), and Hans Hummer, "The Fluidity of Barbarian Identity: The Ethnogenesis of Alemanni and Suebi, AD 200–500," *Early Medieval Europe* 7 (1998): 1–27.

23. Procopius of Caesarea, *History of the Wars* III, ii, 1–6. On the Goths, see Herwig Wolfram, *History of the Goths* (Berkeley, 1987) and, for a more traditional history that does not accept Wolfram's sense of fluidity within the Goths, see Peter Heather, *The Goths* (Oxford, 1996).

24. In Constantine Prophyrogenitus, *Excerpta de Legationibus Romanorum ad Gentes*, Carolus de Boor, ed. (Berlin, 1093), I, p. 135. On the Huns, see Otto Maenchen-Helfen, *The World of the Huns* (Berkeley, 1973); E. A. Thompson, *The Huns* 2ⁿᵈ rev. ed. (Oxford, 1996); and Herwig Wolfram, "The Huns and the Germanic Peoples" in Franz H. Baüml and Marianna D. Birnbaum, eds. *Attila: The Man and his Image* (Budapest, 1993), pp. 16–25.

25. Procopius, III, ii, 4–5.

26. Ammianus Marcellinus, XXII, 5.

27. "*Originem Gothicam fecit esse historiam Romanam.*" Cassidorius *Variae*. 9.25.4–6.

28. Walter Goffart, *The Narrators of Barbarian History (A.D. 550–800): Jordanes, Gregory of Tours, Bede, and Paul the Deacon* (Princeton, 1988), pp. 35–38.

Chapter Three
Barbarians and Other Romans

1. Apuleius, 11, 5.

2. Reinhard Wenskus, *Stammesbildung und Verfassung: das Werden der frühmittelalterlichen Gentes* (Cologne, 1961). Walter Pohl, in "Ethnicity in Early Medieval Studies," *Archaeologia Polona* 29 (1991): p. 41 points out that the term dates back at least to its use in 1912 by H. M. Chadwick.

3. Walter Pohl, "Telling the Difference: Signs of Ethnic Identity," in Walter Pohl with Helmut Reimetz, *Strategies of Distinction: The Construction of Ethnic Communities, 300–800* (Leiden, 1998), pp. 17–69.

4. Velleius Paterculus, *Historiae Romanae*, II, 118, 2.

5. Gerhard Wirth, "Rome and Its Germanic Partners in the Fourth Century," in Walter Pohl, ed., *Kingdoms of the Empire: The Integration of Barbarians in Late Antiquity* (Leiden, 1997), pp. 13–55.

6. See, in general, on the Alamanni, Geuenich, *Geschichte der Alemannen*.

7. Cited in Joachim Werner, "Zur Entstehung der Reihengräberzivilization: Ein Beitrag zur Methode der frühgeschichtlichen Archäologie," *Archaeologia Geographica* I (1950): 23–32, reprinted in Franz Petri, *Siedlung, Sprache und Bevölkerungs-struktur im Frankenreich* (Darmstadt, 1973), p. 294.

Chapter Four
New Barbarians and New Romans

1. Tariat Tekin, *A Grammar of Orkhon Turkic* (Bloomington, 1968), p. 265.

2. Priscus, ed. Carolus Müller, *Fragmenta historicorum Graecorum* IV (Paris, 1851), fr. 8.

3. Priscus, ed. Müller, fr. 39. For an analysis of the ethnic implications of this text, see Peter Heather, "Disappearing and Reappearing Tribes," in Pohl, ed., *Strategies of Distinction*, p. 100.

4. David Frye, *Gallia, Patria, Francia: Ethnic Tradition and Transformation in Gaul*, unpublished Ph.D. dissertation, Duke University, 1991, pp. 89–passim. Although the particular "ethnic" interpretation he places on this material can be disputed, I am grateful to Professor Frye for allowing me to read portions of his dissertation.

5. Ausonius, *Ordo urbium nobilium* 20, Hugh G. Wvelyn White, trans. (Cambridge, MA, 1985), 39–41. See also Frye, *Gallia, Patria, Francia*, p. 104.

6. Ausonius, *Praefatiunculae* 1.5. See Frye, *Gallia, Patria, Francia*, pp. 90–91.

7. Iiro Kajanto, *The Latin Cognomina* (Helsinki, 1965); Frye, *Gallia, Patria, Francia*, pp. 95–96.

8. Frye, *Gallia, Patria, Francia*, pp. 92–93; Sidonius, ed. 8.11.1.

9. Zosimus, *Historia nova*, VI, 5, credited by A. H. M. Jones, *The Later Roman Empire 284–602*, vol. I (Baltimore, 1986), p. 187. See also Herwig Wolfram, *The Roman Empire and Its Germanic Peoples* (Berkeley, 1997), p. 240, who doubts the report, at least as it concerned the British.

10. *Chronica Gallica* anno 452, 133.

11. Salvian, *De gubernatione dei* V 5, 21–23.

12. On this issue, in general, see Patrick Amory, *People and Identity in Ostrogothic Italy 489–554* (Cambridge, 1997), esp. chap. 2, "The Ravenna Government and Ethnographic Ideology: From Civilitas to Bellicositas," pp. 43–85.

13. Amory, *People and Identity*, pp. 63–64, citing, for example, Cassidorus, *Variae* 4.1 and 4.2.

14. Amory, *People and Identity*, p. 73; Var. 8.21.6–7.

15. Amory, *People and Identity*, p. 72.

16. Procopius V, XXV–VI.

17. Procopius, VIII, xxxiv.

Chapter Five
The Last Barbarians?

1. Marius of Avenches, a. 573 MGH AA 11, 238.

2. *Historia Langobardorum* 2,31.

3. *Historia Langobardorum* 2,32.

4. On the various sources that suggest the attraction exercised by the Lombards on at least some elements in Italian society, see Wickham, *Early Medieval Italy,* p. 67.

5. Rothari 367, MGH LL 4. See Brigitte Pohl-Resl, "Legal Practice and Ethnic Identity in Lombard Italy," in Pohl, *Strategies of Distinction: The Construction of Ethnic Communities, 300–800* (Leiden, 1998), p. 209.

6. *Historia Langobardorum* 2, 32.

7. Wickham, *Early Medieval Italy,* pp. 68–69.

8. Liutprand, 91, ed. Bluhme, MGH LL 4. Translation by Katherine Fischer Drew, *The Lombard Laws,* (Philadelphia, 1973) pp. 183–184. See also Pohl-Resl, "Legal Practice and Ethnic Identity," pp. 209–210.

9. Pohl-Resl,"Legal Practice and Ethnic Identity," p. 209.

10. Pohl-Resl, "Legal Practice and Ethnic Identity," p. 210.

11. Ibid.

12. Stephen C. Fanning, "Lombard Arianism Reconsidered," *Speculum* 56 (1981): 241–258.

13. Wickham, *Early Medieval Italy,* pp. 72–73. Wickham is drawing on the data and analysis of Giovanni Tobacco, "Dai possessori dell'età carolingia agli esceritali dell'età longobarda" *Studi medievali* x.1 (1969): 221–268. However, Tobacco doubts that the assimilation of Romans was far advanced. More recently, in his *Struggle for Power in Medieval Italy: Structures of Political Rule* (Cambridge, 1989), Tobacco concedes that "perhaps it is not impossible that at the end of the seventh century, when the conversion of the Lombards to Catholicism was almost complete, their co-existence in the same social class with the remnants of the class of Roman landowners should have led some Romans to accept the judicial tradition of the dominant people...." However, he continues to doubt that there had been any "substantial legal and military assimilation of a free Roman population by the Lombards." (96–97)

14. *Edictus Langobardorum, Aistulfi Leges,* 2, 3. For a translation, see Katherine Fischer Drew, trans. *The Lombard Laws,* p. 228.

15. *Edictus Langobardorum, Aistulfi Leges,* 4. See Drew, *The Lombard Laws,* pp. 228–229.

16. *Codice Diplomatico Longobardo,* ed. Luigi Schiaparelli, I (Rome, 1929), no. 17, p. 48 and no. 20, p. 81.

17. Wolf Liebeschuetz, "Citizen Status and Law," in Pohl, ed., *Strategies of Distinction,* pp. 141–143.

18. Liebeschuetz, "Citizen Status and Law," pp. 139–140; See, in detail, Hagith Sivan, "The Appropriation of Roman Law in Barbarian Hands: Roman-Barbarian Marriage in Visigothic Gaul and Spain," in Pohl, ed., *Strategies of Distinction,* pp. 189–203.

19. Sivan, "The Appropriation of Roman Law," pp. 195–199.

20. Liebeschuetz, "Citizen Status and the Law," p. 149.

21. Liebeschuetz, "Citizen Status and the Law," p. 141.

22. Roger Collins, *Early Medieval Europe* (New York, 1991), p. 145.

23. P. D. King, *Law and Society in the Visigothic Kingdom* (Cambridge, 1972), p. 132.

24. Dietrich Claude, "Remarks about Visigoths and Hispano-Romans in the Seventh Century," citing the work of Volker Bierbrauer and others, in Pohl, ed. *Strategies of Distinction,* p. 119, note 23.

25. King, *Law and Society,* p. 18.

26. *Concilium toletanum* 6, 17, pp. 244–245. See Claude, "Remarks about Visigoths and Hispano-Romans in the Seventh Century," pp. 127–129.

27. King, *Law and Society,* pp. 130–144.

28. Eugen Ewig, "Volkstum und Volksbewußtsein im Frankenreich des 7. Jahrhunderts," in Eugen Ewig, *Spätantikes und fränkisches Gallien,* Hartmut Atsma, ed., vol. I (Munich, 1976), p. 234.

29. Ian Wood, *The Merovingian Kingdoms 450–751* (Harlow, 1994), pp. 108–114.

30. Patrick Wormald, "Lex Scripta and Verbum Regis: Legislation and Germanic Kingship from Euroic to Cnut," in P. H. Sawyer and I. N. Wood, eds., *Early Medieval Kingship* (Leeds, 1977), p. 108.

31. Patrick Amory, "Meaning and Purpose of Ethnic Terminology in Burgundian Laws," *Early Medieval Europe,* 2 (1993): 1–28.

32. Ian Wood, "Ethnicity and the Ethnogenesis of the Burgundians," in Herwig Wolfram and Walter Pohl, eds., *Typen der Ethnogenese unter besonderer Berücksichtigung der Bayern,* vol. I (Vienna, 1990), pp. 55–69.

33. Gregory of Tours, *Libri Historiarum* X,10; Wood, "Ethnicity," p. 55.

34. Ewig, "Volkstum und Volksbewußtsein," p. 251.

35. Walter Goffart, "Foreigners in the Histories of Gregory of Tours," in Walter Goffart, *Rome's Fall and After* (London, 1989), pp. 275–291; and Patrick J. Geary, "Ethnic Identity As a Situational Construct in the Early Middle Ages," *Mitteilungen der anthropologischen Gesellschaft in Wien,* vol. 113 (1983): 15–26.

36. Ewig, "Volkstum und Volksbewußtsein," pp. 247–248.

37. Gregory of Tours, II, 18.

38. Pohl, "Telling the Difference: Signs of Ethnic Identity," p. 37.

39. Henry Mayr-Harting, *The Coming of Christianity to Anglo-Saxon England,* 3rd ed. (Avon, 1991). On the role of the indigenous population in conversion, see Patrick Sims-Williams, *Religion and Literature in Western England, 600–800* (Cambridge, 1990), chap. 3, "Paganism and Christianity," pp. 54–86.

40. Wood, *The Merovingian Kingdoms,* pp. 163–164.

41. Pohl, *Die Awaren. Ein Steppenvolk in Mitteleuropa 567–822 n. Ch.* (Munich, 1988), pp. 18–19.

42. Pohl, "The Role of the Steppe Peoples in Eastern and Central Europe in the First Millennium A.D.," in *Origins of Central Europe,* Przemyslaw Urbanczyk ed. (Warsaw, 1997), pp. 65–78.

43. On the origins of the Slavs, see especially Pohl, *Die Awaren,* pp. 94–128, and Florin Curta, *The Making of the Slavs: History and Archaeology of the Lower Danube Region, ca. 500–700 AD* (Cambridge, 2001).

44. Procopius, *History of the Wars* VII, xiv, 22.

45. Fredegar, 4,48; Pohl, *Die Awaren,* pp. 256–261.

46. Constantine Prophyrogenitus, *De Administrando Imperio,* chaps. 29 and 30.

47. Pohl, *Die Awaren,* p. 266.

48. For a summary of the traditional account, see, for example, John Fine, *The Early Balkans: A Critical Survey from the Sixth to the Late Twelfth Century* (Ann Arbor, 1983), pp. 52–53.

49. Fredegar, 4,72.

50. Miracles of St. Demetrius II, 5.

Chapter Six
Toward New European Peoples

1. On such terminology, see Walter Pohl, "Zur Bedeutung ethnischer Unterscheidungen in der frühen Karolingerzeit," *Studien zur Sachsenforschung* 12 (1999): 193–208, esp. p. 199.

2. On the Bavarian law, see Wilfried Hartmann, "Das Recht," in *Die Bajuwaren von Severin bis Tassilo, 488–788,* H. Dannheimer and H. Dopsch, eds. (Munich, 1988), esp. p. 266; and Joachim Jahn, *Ducatus Baiuvariorum. Das bairische Herzogtum der Agilolfinger* (Stuttgart, 1991), p. 344.

3. See, for example, the grants of "German law" in Poland cited by Robert Bartlett, *The Making of Europe: Conquest, Colonization and Cultural Change 950–1350* (Princeton, 1993), pp. 118 and 130–131.

4. Walter Goffart, in *Narrators of Barbarian History,* shows how little these so-called "national" historians initiated or supported any sort of national history.

5. J. B. Wright and C. A. Hamilton, "Traditions and Transformations: The Phongolo-Mzimkhulu Region in the Late Eighteenth and Early Nineteenth Centuries," in A. Dummy and B. Guest, eds., *Natal and Zululand: From Earliest Times to*

1910: A New History (Pietermaritzburg, 1989), pp. 49–57. See also Carolyn Anne Hamilton, *Terrific Majesty: The Power of Shaka Zulu and the Limits of Historical Invention* (Cambridge, MA, 1998).

6. A. T. Bryant, *Olden Times in Zululand and Natal* (London, 1929) p. viii.

7. Bryant, *Olden Times in Zululand,* p. ix.

8. Bryant, *Olden Times in Zululand,* p. viii.

9. Bryant, *Olden Times in Zululand,* p. x.

10. Bryant, *Olden Times in Zululand,* p. vii–ix.

11. Bryant, *Olden Times in Zululand,* p. 4.

12. Bryant, *Olden Times in Zululand,* p. 17.

13. Bryant, *Olden Times in Zululand,* p. 19.

14. Bryant, *Olden Times in Zululand,* p. ix.

15. Bryant, *Olden Times in Zululand,* p. 101.

16. On the cultural and political backgrounds of four of these early medieval historians, see Walter Goffart, *Narrators of Barbarian History,* who argues that their specific political and religious concerns determined the content and form of their histories.

17. On nineteenth-century sources, both European and African, concerning the great Zulu leader Shaka, see William Worger, "Clothing Dry Bones: The Myth of Shaka," *Journal of African Studies,* vol. 6, no. 3 (1979): 144–158; and Carolyn Anne Hamilton, *Terrific Majesty,* especially chap. 2, "The Origins of the Image of Shaka," pp. 36–71.

18. Wright and Hamilton, "Traditions and Transformations," p. 52.

19. Ibid., p. 53.

Suggestions for Further Reading

Since this book is intended for a general audience and not for scholars, for the most part I have provided in the Notes references to standard ancient and medieval authors and texts simply by giving the title, book, and chapter reference without citing specific editions or translations. A reader who does not know Latin or Greek but who wishes to pursue these sources further would do well to consult one of the translations available for most of the texts, always remembering that, in the words of a professional translator, "every translation is a polite lie."

Two series of excellent translations are readily available for most of these texts. The first are the Loeb Classical Library editions, which provide a translation with the original Latin or Greek on the facing pages. Some of these translations date from the early twentieth century, while others are quite recent. The series includes not only the standard ancient authors but also such important authors of Late Antiquity as Ausonius and Procopius.

The second are Penguin Paperback editions of such authors as Herodotus, Pliny, Livy, Ammianus Marcellinus, Tacitus, and a few medieval texts, such as Gregory of Tours's *Histories*. The University of Pennsylvania Press has published translations of Paul the Deacon's *History of the Lombards* and the Burgundian, Lombard, and Salic law.

Recently, the Liverpool University Press has begun to publish an excellent series titled Translated Texts for Historians, which includes a wide variety of authors from Late Antiquity and the Early Middle Ages not previously available in translation. These include additional works by Gregory of Tours, Cassidorius, and Victor of Vita on the Vandals. The Liverpool series is distributed by the University of Pennsylvania Press and is readily available in paperback.

The literature on contemporary ethnic nationalism and its roots in the nineteenth century is enormous and growing. In addition to the classics—Benedict Anderson, *Imagined Communities* (London: Verso, 1991) and Ernst Gellner, *Nations and Nationalism* (Ithaca, NY: Cornell University Press, 1983)—one can consult with profit Anthony D. Smith, *The Ethnic Origins of Nations* (Oxford: Blackwell, 1986) and Eric J. Hobsbawm, *Nations and Nationalism since 1780* (London: Canto, 1991).

There are numerous histories of Late Antiquity and the Early Middle Ages, but many of these—most unintentionally—are deeply implicated in the kind of nationalist historical narratives this book argues against. Others naturally tend to treat peoples as objective, enduring actors in the stories that they tell, thus unwittingly perpetuating the understanding of peoples first developed in the nineteenth century. Much of the fundamental history of this period is published in continental European languages and not accessible to an English-only audience. Nevertheless, reading across the grain, one can learn much from some of the more recent histories of this period. The following are recent studies that can take an interested reader into this fascinating and insufficiently understood world.

Roger Collins's *Early Medieval Europe* (New York: St. Martin's Press, 1991) is a dense, detailed, political narrative of the period, while Judith Herrin's *The Formation of Christendom* (Princeton: Princeton University Press, 1987) is more of a cultural history. Peter Brown's *The Rise of Western Christendom: Triumph and Diversity AD 200–1000* (Oxford: Blackwell Publishers Inc., 1996) is a synthetic and culturally oriented survey of the transformation of Late Antiquity and the early medieval period. *Fifth-Century Gaul: A Crisis of Identity?*, edited by John Drinkwater and Hugh Elton (Cambridge: Cambridge University Press, 1992), draws together many of the currently debated issues about Western European society and polity at the end of Antiquity. Herwig Wolfram's *The Roman Empire and Its Germanic Peoples* (Berkeley and Los Angeles: University of California Press, 1997) is the best introduction to the process of late Antique ethnogenesis in any language.

Individual "peoples" have found their own historians. The finest example of the new approach to understanding the constitutional nature of peoples in the period is Herwig Wolfram's *History of the Goths* (Berkeley: University of California Press, 1988). Ian Wood's *The Merovingian Kingdoms* (London: Longman, 1994) does a fine job of introducing the reader to Frankish history. A British series, titled *Peoples of Europe* published by Blackwell Publishers Ltd., presents short, accessible histories of Europe's peoples, "from their origins in prehistory to the present day." Some, but by no means all the volumes in the series have not broken free of older understandings of ethnicity and may have a tendency to objectify the "peoples" and overstate their continuity.

Exciting and fundamental work on ethnicity has been done by an international collaborative project of the European Science Foundation, titled the Transformation of the Roman World. A great number of volumes emerging from this project are planned. Among those that have already appeared are Walter Pohl, ed. *Kingdoms of the Empire: The Integration of Barbarians in Late Antiquity* (Leiden: Brill, 1997) and Walter Pohl with Helmut Reimitz, eds., *Strategies of Distinction: The Construction of Ethnic Identity Communities 300–800* (Leiden: Brill, 1998).

Finally, a number of younger scholars have begun to re-evaluate aspects of the received tradition of national history in Central and Eastern Europe. Among these are Patrick Amory's *People and Identity in Ostrogothic Italy 489–554* (Cambridge: Cambridge University Press, 1997), one of the most ambitious attempts to demonstrate the complex realities of early medieval identity, and Florin Curta's *The Making of the Slavs: History and Archaeology of the Lower Danube Region, Ca. 500–700* (Cambridge: Cambridge University Press, 2001). One can only hope that, in the years to come, this brief bibliography will need to be greatly expanded as historians in Europe, North America, and Asia will continue to untangle the myth of nations.

187

Index